How to Grow Marijuana & CBD Hemp Oil

(Two Book Box Set)

Tom Whistler

original author of this work can be in any fashion deemed liable for any hardship or damages that may befall them after undertaking information described herein.

Additionally, the information found on the following pages is intended for informational purposes only and should thus be considered, universal. As befitting its nature, the information presented is without assurance regarding its continued validity or interim quality. Trademarks that mentioned are done without written consent and can in no way be considered an endorsement from the trademark holder.

Table of Contents

How to Grow Marijuana

From Seed to Harvest - Complete Step by Step Guide for Beginners

Introduction

I want to thank you and congratulate you for purchasing the book, *"How to Grow Marijuana: From Seed to Harvest - Complete Step by Step Guide for Beginners"*.

This book contains proven steps and strategies on how to cultivate marijuana for your personal medicinal and recreational use. This is suitable for beginners and for those who have tried before but were dissatisfied with the results.

The cultivation and consumption of the cannabis plant has been controversial for decades. Despite the widespread and long-standing prohibition in many countries around the world, the said practices were kept. Growers and users used to hide their deeds. Their actions may be illegal but they were not necessarily immoral, unethical or destructive. With the discovery of the different medicinal properties of marijuana, the barriers against the cultivation and consumption are becoming a thing of the past.

The legalization of growing and using marijuana in several states in the US and in many parts of the world is a success of those who took the risk of applying and maintaining the practices. Cultivating your own cannabis plants entails voicing your support for the political movement and enjoying your right to do it. The best part of it all is that you can have a homegrown natural remedy to a variety of health conditions.

It is easy to understand if you perceive the challenge of growing the plant as intimidating. It might be your first foray into the world of gardening. You might not know how and where to start. With this book, you will be able to know about the basics of marijuana cultivation such as:

- Steps in marijuana cultivation

- Seed selection

- Seed germination methods

- Requirements and plant care for outdoor marijuana cultivation

- Requirements and plant care for indoor marijuana cultivation

- Common marijuana plant problems and their solutions

- Pest control and prevention

- Proper harvesting

Plus, you will also know more about the different medical benefits you may get from marijuana. Hint: There is more to it than just the high!

Thanks again for purchasing this book, I hope you enjoy it!

Chapter 1: Cannabis Cultivation for Yourself, by Yourself

Cannabis will go down in history as one of the most controversial plants of all time. More popularly known as marijuana, the plant is notorious for being the source of a substance that many people abuse for psychoactive effects. On the other side, there are researchers, health care professionals, manufacturers and tribesmen who back up the cultivation and use of the plant for medical, industrial and cultural purposes.

In many countries, it is still illegal to grow, possess, sell and utilize cannabis. However, the discovery of its medicinal properties, especially for the management of some cancers and behavioral disorders, has paved the way for the legalization of medical marijuana in countries such as Canada, Colombia, Chile, Israel, Spain, Belgium, Austria, Finland, Netherlands, United Kingdom and Czech Republic. Marijuana use, be it recreational or medical, is still prohibited under the US federal law but 29 states have already legalized medical marijuana as of 2016 and many are expected to follow suit.

The industrial sector benefits from the cultivation of the plant as well. All the species under the genus Cannabis used for manufacturing are known collectively as hemp or industrial hemp. It is often utilized for the production of fuel, paper, textiles, biodegradable plastics and construction materials. Aside from its multiple industrial uses, the plant is valued for requiring little to no harmful chemicals for its cultivation and processing. That means it is not only good for the body but for the environment as well.

The first use of marijuana dates back to the ancient times. It has been integrated into different rituals and festivities since then. Take the *Holi* festival in India and Nepal as an example. During the festivities, people therein consume *bhang*, a cannabis derivative containing flowers from the plant.

It is believed that Indian traders brought the plant to Egyptians, and from there, the latter introduced it to other Africans. Slaves who were brought to the Americas were the ones who later on spread the practice of marijuana cultivation and consumption in the two continents.

In spite of its medical, industrial and cultural significance, many people still frown upon the recreational use of marijuana. This, along with the laws banning the use of recreational marijuana, prompted avid users to engage further in illicit trades, covert pot sessions and illegal cultivation of the plant. However, now that the laws prohibiting marijuana cultivation and use have been somewhat relaxed or even lifted in many places, growing your own cannabis plant is worth a try if you are living in a state or country where it is legal.

Why Cultivate

Right now, several big companies are investing millions of money for further research about the plant and its potential uses. Individual marijuana cultivation helps prevent the possible monopoly of the big companies towards the uses of the plant. The practice is also virtuous in many other ways.

If you, or a loved one has a prescription for medicinal marijuana, having your own plant means there is always a remedy nearby. Depending on the laws governing your area, you may also use your plant for self-medication. Get to know the medical benefits of the plant in the next chapter.

Aside from availability, growing your own marijuana plant gives you an assurance of clean produce. You are the only one who knows how your plant is handled and what chemicals are used in your plant. This aspect is valuable if you are using the plant for treatment or if you are into organic farming.

Furthermore, individual and small-scale growers of marijuana attest to the affordability of cultivating the plant and preparing its derivatives. A variety of factors contributed to the high costs of joint and other marijuana products. Topping the list would be the illegal activities involved. Big time marijuana dealers have to bribe government officials in various parts of the world to continue their illegal cultivation, production and sale of the products. The shipment costs are another factor. Keep in mind, the limited number of companies legally allowed to provide medical marijuana. The lack of stiff competition enables them to dictate the price of the useful product. Growing your marijuana and preparing a medicine or joint may require your time, effort and money but it is more affordable than buying it from a dealer.

Legal Considerations

Cannabis cultivation is bound to be a worthwhile activity, except if it is still illegal in your place. Before you jump into the bandwagon, refer to the laws governing marijuana cultivation in your place. Be sure to check the basic requirements and limitations set by the authorities. You have to know all the laws, rules and regulations applicable to marijuana cultivation in your place. Apart from state, federal and national laws, you have to be mindful of laws in your county and city/municipality. If you are renting and/or living in a condominium, you might need to talk to your landlord or building manager about your plan.

The requirements and limitations differ from one place to another. In some states in the US, you have to get a license to cultivate marijuana. If you are going to grow marijuana for trade, you need to apply for a separate permit to do so. Additionally, you must be at least 21 years old. The number of plants you can grow may also be limited. Such is the case in Denver, Colorado. In some states in the US, growers can only grow and cultivate marijuana in an enclosed area.

Verifying the legality of marijuana cultivation and getting documents to do so may be a time-consuming and tedious task. However, this will spare you from possible criminal liabilities, discrimination and headaches later on. It will also help condition your mind and body that you are going to carry out a serious and worthwhile venture.

Chapter 2: Medical Benefits of Marijuana

Cannabis has been utilized as a medicinal plant for centuries. You, as well as the majority of medical and recreational users, can attest that the use of such can improve overall feeling of wellness. If you find yourself struggling with the cultivation later on, try to remember the different medical benefits you can get from it.

Cannabinoids are the main forces behind the medical benefits of marijuana. These are also the same compounds that make pot smoking addicting. Unlike other abused substances though, the body is optimized to receive the said compounds thanks to the cannabinoid receptors that are already in the human body even before birth. Even breast milk, which serves as the main source of nutrients for newborns, are packed with the compounds similar to those from marijuana. As the name suggests, the aforementioned receptors and the cannabinoid compounds bind. Their binding brings about a myriad of health benefits such as:

Mood Improvement

Most people who turn to recreational marijuana are after the high the substance can provide. Being on high offers a happy and relaxed feeling. Marijuana indeed has mood stabilizing

13

properties which benefit those who experience typical to extreme mood swings. Some studies even suggest that medical marijuana has great potential in controlling violent mood swings of people with autism.

Pain Management

Marijuana is also popular for the management of different body aches. It can help alleviate headaches and back pain. In addition, some people who suffer from chronic pain report less frequent and/or less intense discomfort after using cannabis derivatives.

Appetite Modulation

Some marijuana strains can trigger the so-called munchies or those sudden bursts of hunger. This only proves that the consumption of cannabis derivatives can affect digestion. However, not all strains can cause munchies. Other strains, as proven in studies, can actually help modulate appetite. The appetite modulating properties of marijuana are so noteworthy that it is even being studied and used for the management of anorexia and other eating disorders.

Weight Loss

It might seem counterintuitive that marijuana use can bring about munchies and weight loss. After all, plenty of weight loss supplements brag about the fat-burning and appetite-suppressing properties of their ingredients. However, the sudden bursts of hunger from marijuana do not seem to make all users obese. In contrast, majority of users are far from being overweight. There are different factors that affect the weight of users. These are not just about the medical properties of the plant but the behavior of users as well. Some go for pot smoking for comfort while others turn to binge eating.

Sleep Enhancement

Some people regard marijuana as a natural remedy for sleeping problems such as insomnia and sleep apnea. Using it before bedtime can keep nightmares at bay. Aged cannabis derivatives provide better sleep than newly processed ones. It is also helpful to add other natural, complementary sleeping remedies to marijuana instead of over-the-counter sleeping pills. However, this is not advisable to young ones who face sleeping difficulties.

Muscle Relaxation

In some studies, marijuana consumption is effective in relieving muscle spasms and pain for both humans and animals. Some proponents even say that this natural muscle relaxant is better than the ones manufactured by big pharmaceutical companies. It is best to combine marijuana with massages and other remedies that do not involve mass produced pills.

Diabetes Treatment and Risk Reduction

Marijuana use can help improve insulin sensitivity and enhance blood sugar regulation as some studies proved. These, along with the weight loss benefits, are especially helpful to those with diabetes or at risk of developing the chronic condition due to their lifestyle or genetics.

Phobia Management

Some health care professionals warn about the possible paranoia or anxiety that marijuana consumption can cause. However, many users report that they are able to feel relief for their anxiety, paranoia and phobia. Some people have clinical phobias that are so disruptive that they call for medicines to help them deal with day-to-day living. Many of them turn to marijuana as an alternative and are satisfied by how their decision turns out.

Neuroprotection

The compounds from marijuana affect the brain in many ways. The psychoactive effects are the most controversial of all. These are partly the cause of on-going debates on marijuana legalization. Some antis claim that the legalization is not worth the risk due to the said effects. Pros, on the other hand, highlight the neuroprotective properties of cannabis and its potential in treating Alzheimer's disease, Parkinson's disease and other brain conditions.

Depression Management

Medical marijuana is also seen as a good addition to depression management. It is partly due to its mood stabilizing properties. Aside from mood improvement, it may alleviate fatigue and disinterest that clinically depressed individuals tend to suffer from. However, recreational marijuana may only bring about temporary relief for depression and may trigger addiction instead to some users.

Glaucoma Treatment

Marijuana has the ability to regulate the pressure in the eye which is beneficial in the prevention and treatment of glaucoma. The vasodilation and neuroprotection it offers also helps lower down the risk of vision loss. Smoking pot may treat glaucoma but it is quite time-consuming and dangerous for the lungs. Pills and injections are better and safer alternatives but they require medical expertise.

Cancer Treatment

Cancer patients can benefit from medical marijuana in different ways. Some proponents believed that it could kill cancer cells. While there are few conclusive studies to prove so, it is widely recognized that it helps relieve the side effects of chemotherapy such as pain, nausea, vomiting and appetite loss.

While beneficial in many ways, excessive consumption of marijuana can bring about some health problems. Chills, heavy limbs, burning eyes, extreme dry mouth, and severe paranoia are some of the signs and symptoms of marijuana overdose. The good thing is that the overdosing is not likely to kill you. Nevertheless, you need to relax, stay hydrated and talk to your health care provider when you experience the aforementioned signs and symptoms.

Plenty of medical benefits from marijuana use are yet to be explored, but the on-going studies are very promising. Before the big pharmaceutical companies beat you to it, make sure you learn how to cultivate your own clean and natural remedy.

Chapter 3: Steps in Marijuana Cultivation

Cultivation in general can be quite intimidating if it is your first time. The good thing is that you can master this skill given some time and practice. Aside from honing your gardening skills, you get the chance to reap the fruits of your hard work.

It will take months before you can harvest your own marijuana produce. There is also the possibility that you might not reap anything at all. But that is okay. You can simply start again.

Marijuana cultivation requires time, effort and commitment. It seems hard at first but learning it and harvesting your produce later on will make it fun and worthwhile. Additionally, you will have a better view on gardening as a whole.

There are different ways to grow marijuana and you have to consider a couple of things along the way. But, below are key steps applicable to all techniques of marijuana cultivation.

Step 1: Determine your specific purpose for planting.

Personal consumption is probably your main reason. You have to state though whether it is for medication, recreation or both. Determine the number of users as well. Decide the number of plants you want to grow based on your purpose for planting.

Step 2: Comply with the applicable laws, rules and regulations about planting marijuana in your place.

Search online and visit government websites concerning the cultivation and use of marijuana in your state and country. Read applicable laws, and take note of the requirements and limitations. Talk to your landlord or building manager if you live in an apartment or condominium. Meet the basic legal requirements (such as license or permit) before you even start planting. Always keep in mind the limitations as well. If the law says you can only plant up to 10 marijuana plants, then you should only grow 10 or less. Also, be on the lookout for the recommended techniques and designs. In some state laws, marijuana cultivation should only be done in an enclosed and secured area to keep minors away.

Step 3: Choose whether to grow your marijuana plants outdoors or indoors.

You should first know what is allowed or recommended in your area before deciding which one to apply. Each technique has its fair share of advantages and disadvantages. You will know more about the best application of each technique in the next chapters. Outdoor cultivation and indoor cultivation with soil as medium remain the most suitable for first-time growers. Once you have mastered one or both of the said methods, you can try out hydroponic gardening which is becoming more popular recently, not just for marijuana cultivation but for growing other crops.

Step 4: Prepare your garden or grow room.

As usual, refer to the recommended designs or the garden requirements if there are any. You have to consider three things for your garden: location, growing medium, and plant needs. Pick the most suitable place in your garden or in your home for your marijuana garden or grow room. As a beginner, soil is the best planting medium you can use, but there are many other growing mediums out there. For your plant needs, you have to focus on lights, water and nutrients. For indoor marijuana cultivation, you may also need to control temperature, humidity, smell and many other aspects.

Step 5: Select your seeds.

Seed selection is one of the most enjoyable parts of marijuana cultivation. There are only three species under the genus Cannabis, but you can also choose from many hybrids that marijuana enthusiasts developed in the previous years. The strains come in fun, mysterious and interesting names. It can get pretty confusing as the names of the strains may be totally unrelated to their advantageous properties.

Before you buy seeds, search for the different strains online. You need to consider different things when it comes to seed selection. As a beginner, you have to research which strains are easy to cultivate and highly resilient. Additionally, get to know the best strains for your medial condition if you are planning to grow marijuana for treatment. You should also weigh on the suitability of strains for outdoor or indoor cultivation. It pays to know the quantity and quality of their expected yield as well.

After choosing the strains you want to buy, it is time to look for a supplier. You can buy from a physical or online store. You may also refer to individual breeders. Always verify the legitimacy of your supplier to guarantee that you are purchasing the right strain for your planting goals.

Step 6: Germinate your seeds.

Germination is the process of allowing your seeds to sprout. It will take a few days to a week. There are various methods to do so. Each method requires a different set of materials. There are also conditions that you need to meet to make sure that seed germination takes place. In some methods, you might need to transplant and that calls for additional guidelines you have to follow.

Step 7: Take care of your plants. This involves:

- *Providing light, water and nutrients*

- *Training your plants*

- *Preventing and managing possible plant problems and pest infestation*

Proper plant care differs for each growing phase. Marijuana

plants undergo four growing phases and these are: seedling phase, vegetative phase, pre-flowering phase, and flowering phase. Aside from the phase, proper plant care is also different between outdoor and indoor cultivation. This step will take the most time. It is bound to be the most difficult as well.

Step 8: Harvest your produce.

The best part of growing a plant is being able to harvest and use the fruits of your labor, or in the case of marijuana, the flowers. You do not need a big laboratory or a degree to prepare your own natural remedy out of marijuana. There are basic preparations you can try.

The abovementioned steps are just an overview of the actual cultivation process. More detailed guidelines are provided in the next chapters. Now that you are familiar with the steps, you can proceed with choosing your seeds.

Chapter 4: Seed Selection to Seed Germination

Seed selection in marijuana cultivation is a lot more complex than you think. Some books are solely dedicated for that subject alone. As a beginner and an individual grower, you do not have to scour such books for now. If you become interested with experimenting and breeding different marijuana seeds, you might want to invest in a book that offers detailed information about them. For the meantime, you simply have to focus on the best seeds for beginners.

In this chapter, you will know about the basics of seed selection and the methods of seed germination. However, you have to remember that you need to prepare your garden first before doing your seed hunt. Your garden and the materials should be ready so you can focus on the seed germination later on. Get to know the ways to prepare your garden in the next chapters.

Types/Species

Cannabis is a member of the Cannabaceae family, which also includes plants that are used as ornaments. There are three classifications/species of cannabis, but there are also hybrids. The three main species are as follows:

Cannabis indica – This one is native to Central Asia. This one is ideal for indoor cultivation as it usually does not go beyond 4 feet. Body relaxation is among the noteworthy health benefits from this species.

Cannabis sativa – This species is native to Southeast Asia. Outdoor cultivation is the most suitable technique for this species because it tends to grow beyond 4 feet. Mood improvement is one of the notable medical benefits from this species.

Cannabis ruderalis – This species is native to Eastern Europe. It grows in the wild which makes it practically a low-maintenance plant. However, it has low tetrahydrocannabinol or THC (the main cannabinoid in cannabis) content and it cannot be used for smoking. Because of this, its seeds are rarely sold to individual growers.

Hybrids – You can get these from seed banks and individual breeders. These are the best option if you want to get the benefits from two different Cannabis species. Even strains from *C. ruderalis* plants may be sought for hybrids because even though they are less therapeutic than other species, they tend to be highly resilient.

Females versus Males

Marijuana plants are made up of females and males. The basic difference between the two is their flowers. The flowers from male marijuana plants have no value to individual growers who simply want the plants for medication and relaxation. You should only let males develop if you want to reap seeds for future cultivations, for breeding strains, or for sale.

However, the gender of a marijuana seed is not predetermined like that of humans or animals. Each seed is assumed to be 50% female and 50% male. If you stumble upon charts detailing the physical differences of female and male marijuana seeds, they are most likely to be false.

Right now, feminized seeds are your best bet at getting the useful marijuana flowers. These seeds are specifically bred to be 99% females. But, there is a remaining 1% chance that they can turn into hermaphrodites or develop male-like features. This means they will not provide the flowers you are expecting. To prevent this from happening, make sure your marijuana plants are never subjected to stressful conditions.

Additionally, you need to be on the lookout for the early signs of male marijuana plants even if you used feminized seeds. The surest way to find out whether the seeds are male or female is to wait for their flowers to bloom. However, you cannot afford to do that as the male buds have pollens and these may pollinate or fertilize the female buds, causing the latter to form seeds and rendering them unusable for treatment or relaxation.

The right way to manage a possible male marijuana plant is to wait until it goes to the pre-flowering phase. This comes after the vegetative phase or around the sixth week of the plant since germination. The vegetative phase can be likened to childhood while pre-flowering is to puberty. In the former, the plant just gets thicker stems, develops more and bigger leaves, and grows taller. In the pre-flowering phase, it develops buds, which are attached to its main stem, near the meeting point of the leaves and stem. For females, the buds have two or more white hairs, which are referred as pistils. For males, the buds have the so-called balls which are actually pollen sacs. Remove the plant with the spherical buds early on to prevent the pollen sacs from bursting and spreading their contents to female marijuana plants.

Auto-Flowering Seeds

When you shop for marijuana seeds, you will encounter the term auto-flowering seeds. These are worth considering if you are going to cultivate multiple plants or if you just want to harvest the flowers sooner. It takes 24 hours of light for a regular marijuana seed to grow and 12-hour light cycle for it to flower. In contrast, a marijuana plant from an auto-flowering seed may flower even without 12 hours of darkness like that for regular marijuana plants. As long as there is at least 12 hours of light each day, the plant may flower. You do not need to adjust the lighting or separate the seedling, vegetating and flowering plants. You do not have to wait long for it to produce flowers as well. You can enjoy your harvest after 2 to 3 months.

Best Strains for Beginners

Some marijuana strains are relatively easy to grow and resilient. These are the recommended options for beginners. Strains that flower fast and produce a high yield require utmost care and attention to grow. Many of these are unable to tolerate high-stress conditions, and so they might not make good choices for first-time growers who are bound to commit mistakes as part of the learning process. You can experiment with high-yielding, auto-flowering, highly potent and other more beneficial strains later on, but for now, focus on strains you might be able to grow even with your limited gardening skills.

The best strains for beginners are as follows:

- Blue Cheese – known for its buds that are stickier than normal ones. This strain is suitable for indoor gardening because it can grow well in tight spaces and under LED lights. It also has high resistance against mold and other plant problems. It can withstand overwatering and under-watering, too.

- Jack Herer – named after a pioneer in marijuana legalization. This one thrives whether cultivated outdoors or indoors. It also has a compact size that makes it an ideal choice for growers who want to keep their planting venture discreet.

- Northern Light – notable for being less smelly as compared to most strains. This is perfect for aspiring growers living in apartments, condominiums or any other buildings where the proximity and presence of marijuana plants may irritate neighbors. Plants from this strain can also withstand less than ideal temperatures and excessive watering.

- Skunk – regarded as one of the classics. It may be grown on soil or soil-less growing mediums (in the case of hydroponics). It can grow even when given less attention. Unlike other strains, it does not stretch much when it develops flowers.

- White Widow – one of the all-time favorites out there. It is unclear how this strain came to be, but most of the leading seed banks today offer this. It is much loved for its potency, clean taste, energizing high, and hardiness as a plant. It can be grown indoors and outdoors, even in places such as Scandinavia and UK where the climate is not ideal for the regular marijuana plant.

These are just recommendations. You can still ditch these if you find another resilient and low-maintenance strain of marijuana.

Possible Sources of Seeds

You have three possible sources of marijuana seeds: physical stores, online stores and individual breeders. Physical stores that offer these seeds are still quite rare in many parts of the world. Hence, buying from online stores and individual breeders are more sensible.

Online stores (or seed banks as they are called in the cannabis community) are well-known for the numerous strains they offer. They offer original strains along with their respective versions of the classics. Compared to individual breeders, online seed banks are more reliable when providing auto-flowering and feminized seeds. They give tips on how to grow them as well. Below are the steps in buying marijuana seeds online:

- Make a list of reliable seed banks by visiting forums, reading reviews and asking marijuana growers amongst your friends.

- Get to know the delivery methods that they employ. Look for problems that previous buyers might have encountered. These problems may include blockage in borders or confiscation by the authorities.

- Simplify your list by removing seed banks that do not cater to your area.

- Go to the websites of the seed banks on your list.

- Check their available strains. See if they have the ones recommended for beginners. Some top seed banks offer more variants of the said strains which could be from their own in-house breeders or from their reliable partners.

- Before you place an order, look at the payment options along with the discounts you can avail. The three main options are cash, credit cards and online payment systems like PayPal. Some let you pay using bitcoins. PayPal gives the best online consumer protection but they do not allow transactions involving marijuana seeds and products on their system. Pay using cash or credit card with discretion. If you have issues with this, you may send an email or message your prospective provider on their website about other payment options.

- Once you have settled your issues with payment option, you may now proceed to placing an order. Indicate the number of seeds you want to buy. Provide your delivery information and pay using your preferred option. Wait for the confirmation of your order. Take note of the expected delivery date.

- Wait until your seeds get delivered. If your order did not arrive on the expected delivery date, contact the seed bank. Strict border controls might have something to do with this. In any case, a reputable seed bank will try to replace it.

If the idea of buying marijuana seeds online scares you, you can always go for local individual breeders. You can refer to your friends who use and grow marijuana for recommendations. The advantages of buying seeds from a local supplier are being able to meet up with him and see the seeds before payment. There is no need for you to enter personal information online. The downside is that the number of strains you can choose from is quite limited, but at least you are assured that you can get seeds right away.

Seed Inspection

Once the seeds you ordered online arrive or if you grab the chance to see them before buying them, try to get rid of unhealthy ones as they are not likely to germinate. First, you have to separate the healthy seeds. A healthy marijuana seed has a shape of a teardrop, about 3/16th inch long and about 1/8th inch wide. Its shell is brown with some darker stripes. In contrast, unhealthy seeds are tiny, soft, whitish, yellowish or greenish.

Ideally, healthy seeds should grow into strong plants. However, veteran growers know that the quality of the seed has less to do with the future health of the plants. As long as the seeds are able to germinate, then everything is fine. The way you care for your plants is a more important factor in ensuring their good health.

Seed Germination

Seed germination is a simple and fun chore but it is also easy to make mistakes in this task. You have to be gentle as the seeds are vulnerable. You should also learn how to wait patiently. Do not go checking on them every minute or every hour after leaving them to sprout. Depending on the germinating conditions and method used, they can sprout within 2 to 7 days. You should do this on springtime so your plants can take advantage of more summer days later on. You can choose one from the four germination methods below:

Method 1: Starter Cube

Marijuana seeds do not come cheap so you do not want to waste any of yours. For beginners like you, using starter cubes to germinate your seeds is highly recommended. The success rate of this method is the highest of the bunch. Below are the steps to germinate using starter cubes:

- Buy a pack of starter cubes that is ideal for your growing technique. (Some are not suitable for hydroponic cultivation so shop wisely.)

- Prepare the starter cubes as instructed in the packaging. Some require getting soaked in water while others may be used without any special preparation at all.

33

- After that, place each seed in its own starter cube. There is already a precut hole in each cube. All you have to do is put the seed in the hole. Close the hole by pinching it gently.

- Water as directed in the packaging of the started cubes.

Your seeds are likely to sprout after one to three days in this method. The next step is to transplant your seedlings in a bigger container. Or, you may plant the entire starter cube directly on your main growing medium. Just make sure the starter cubes you use are biodegradable.

Keep in mind to transplant with the tiny white taproot facing downwards. The growing medium should be moist as well. These apply to all seedlings regardless of the germination methods employed.

Method 2: Glass of Water

Seed germination using a glass of water is cheaper than using starter cubes. Another good thing about this method is that it can wake up old seeds and make them viable for planting again. Below are the steps to germinate using a glass of water.

- Get a small, transparent drinking glass and fill it with slightly warm water.

- Soak your seeds in the glass of water for 24 to 32 hours.

- Prepare your growing medium while you wait.

Viable seeds will float and sink afterwards. Each of these seeds will have tiny white taproot. Transplant them if it has been 24 hours since you soak them. Do not soak them beyond 32 hours as they might drown and not germinate at all. If some do not germinate, try using other germination methods.

Method 3: Paper Towel

Using paper towel is another low-cost germination method. However, this can get a little risky. Always remember to be gentle and let your seeds sprout in peace. Below are the steps to geminate using a paper towel:

- Get a piece of paper towel and two plates. Place the piece of paper towel in one of the plates. Wet the half of the paper towel.

- Put the seeds on the moistened part of the paper towel and then fold it. Cover it with the other plate. This keeps the moisture inside. Without it, the seeds will dry and die.

- Check for sprouts every 12 hours. Prepare your growing medium as you wait.

It may take one to four days before the seeds sprout. Older seeds may take longer than that. Before you transplant a seedling, create a hole (about 1 inch deep) in your growing medium.

Method 4: Main Growing Medium

The three methods above involve transplanting seedlings but you do not have to do that if you germinate your seeds directly on your main growing medium. With this method, you will not end up shocking and hurting your seedlings as you transplant them. However, the germination rate for this method is not as good as the others. There is also the possibility that the seeds might get stepped on and crushed when left to sprout outdoors. If you still want to take the risk, below are the steps to germinate using your main growing medium:

- Prepare your growing medium. It is either soil or soil-less (such as coco coir). It may be potted or not.

- Your seeds need warmth to germinate. You can fulfill this need by placing a heating pad or installing a light near your growing medium.

- Moisten your growing medium and create holes as many as your seeds and about 1 inch deep.

- Place one seed in each hole. For outdoor germination, the seeds should be about 3 to 5 feet away from each other. For indoor germination, one seed per pot is enough.

- Keep the growing medium moist but not too wet as the seeds might drown.

- Allow your seeds to grow.

If it has been 10 days since you planted the seeds and no taproots have come out, it is safe to assume that they already died. That makes the germination attempt a waste of time and money. To help ensure that few of your seeds survive and become seedlings, employ two or more germination methods.

Chapter 5: Outdoor Cultivation

Cannabis has thrived in the outdoors for hundreds of years. As an aspiring grower, you should be able to try outdoor cultivation at least once. Perhaps, the main factors that can stop you from doing so include, the law, the lack of outdoor space and the thought of kids, pets or someone else messing up your marijuana plants. If you are allowed and have the space to do so, then try it. Regarding kids, pets or other persons who might mess up your home plantation, you can always set up a fence to protect your plants from intrusion.

There are many benefits to outdoor marijuana cultivation. With this method, you do not need to buy pots unless you are going to do it in your veranda or roof deck. You can take advantage of sunlight, rainwater and carbon dioxide as well. This also allows you to apply organic farming methods that are organic. All of these make outdoor cultivation less expensive than indoor cultivation.

Cannabis plants are hardy thanks to their being grown in the wild for years so the preparation of your planting site should not be that hard. Another good thing about this is that you can yield more because you can use plants with better foliage. With such, the leaves can undergo photosynthesis that will provide the plant with more energy to produce the flowers later on.

Remember that it is called a weed for a reason. It can grow nearly in the most random of places and sometimes, in the most random of times. The derivatives from outdoor marijuana plants are also known to have better taste and aroma.

To reap the benefits of outdoor marijuana cultivation, you have to spend much time on garden preparation. Getting all your gears ready makes the latter steps of cultivation easier and quicker.

Garden Preparation

It is best to start your garden preparation during early springtime. Make it a part of your annual spring cleaning. Instead of just de-cluttering your home, you should also get rid of the garden waste that the previous season left by on your yard. Once you are done with a general cleanup of your yard. It is time to choose a spot for your mini marijuana plantation.

Location

You should pick a location where your marijuana plants will receive sunlight the most. Therefore, areas near or under the trees or the awnings of your home are not ideal. Additionally, the location should be away from areas where there is standing water. The plants will be under high stress if you do so. Aside from that, standing water may attract pests. You should also consider the spacing between your plants (3 to 5 feet away from each other). This is to allow your plants to grow freely and to allow you to move between them with so much ease. You should plan and set up drainage for your garden when you are done picking the right location.

If you are setting up your garden in a veranda or roof deck, make sure your plants will be elevated. The flooring therein, especially if it is tiles, may be too warm that it may put the roots of your marijuana plants in high stress. You can elevate your plants by setting a platform using wood since the material is a good insulator of heat. You can simply create a rectangular box and drill holes where you will place the pots. Coat your wooden platform with a water-resistant finish. Make sure there are trays or saucers below the pots. These are meant to catch run-off water from the potted plants.

Soil

The first thing you need to do is to get rid of grasses or weeds on your planting location. The sight of these organisms might mean trouble but their presence actually indicates that the site is good for marijuana plants. If you have other valued plants in it, transfer it somewhere else. Use a rake to further remove debris in the area. You do not want the possibility of a random piece of broken glass blocking or hurting the root of your upcoming marijuana plants.

Getting your soil ready requires checking its pH level. You can buy a soil testing kit from most gardening stores to know the pH level of your soil. There is no such thing as perfect soil for marijuana cultivation but the ideal pH level of your soil should fall within 5.8 to 6.5.

If the pH level of your soil is not within the said range, you have to improve it by adding compost and other organic fertilizers such as bonemeal, bloodmeal, worm castings, aged manure and bat guano. You may add some biodegradable mulch as well. Chemical fertilizers are more readily available but they can hurt your soil in the long run, preventing you to plant regularly. Once your soil gets polluted, you have to let it rest for a while and treat it with organic soil amendments.

The soil type in your yard matters as well. The soil testing kit you are going to buy is likely to have a tool that can help you know whether your soil is clay, sand or loam. You can simply rely on your observation, too. Clay tends to stick together while sand is too loose. Loamy soil is the most ideal because it may stick together but it drains well which is highly preferred by marijuana plants. Loam contains silt, sand, clay and organic matter.

To find out what kind of soil you have, grab a fistful of soil and squeeze it. If it tends to form a ball, it is probably clay and you might need to boost the amount of silt, sand and organic matter in your soil. If it tends to crumble, it is probably sand and you might have to add clay, silt and organic matter to balance it.

When you are done treating it, pour water in your soil. If it drains well yet remains moist, you have achieved the type of soil conducive for your marijuana cultivation.

Water Supply

Marijuana plants require lots of water in order to thrive. You will not have much problem if you live in a place where it rains a lot. If it rarely rains in your place even in springtime, you should buy an extensive hose or place a water faucet nearby. It pays to have a stream or other bodies of water near your place as well. You can get water from the bodies of water for free but it takes a lot of time and effort.

Protection

Your outdoor marijuana plants have three main enemies: wind, animals and humans. There is nothing much you can do to control the wind but if there is a hilly side in your place, you may use such as a natural shield against wind. If there are no hills, you have no other choice but to set up a fence. This does not only protect your plants against wind but possibly against large animals and humans as well.

That is not enough though. You need to surround your mini marijuana plantation with thorny bushes to prevent small animals like rabbits from messing up your garden. You may also plant other taller plants such as maize. Elderberry and bamboo are both good shields for marijuana plants as well.

Once everything is ready, you can start your hunt for the best strains for outdoor marijuana cultivation. While waiting for your seeds, decide the germination methods you have to employ. Pick at least two. For outdoor cultivation, you might want to germinate some of your seeds directly on the grounds. If you are opting for starter cubes, purchase them before you buy seeds.

After germinating some seeds indoors, you can transfer them to pots for a while. Let them grow indoors first while the outdoor seeds remain. Keep their soil moist but not too wet or too soaking. For the indoor seedlings, give them 24 hours of light. Transfer them outdoors after 3 to 4 weeks.

Plant Care

After transplanting the seedlings, you are bound to face the most tiring part of marijuana cultivation. This requires you to be observant of the way you handle your plants and the way they respond to care you provide.

Vegetative Phase

After the seedling phase, your plants will enter the so-called vegetative phase. It is usually on the second month after germination. In this phase, the plants will do nothing but grow more leaves and stems. They are going to need lots of water, nutrients and sunlight.

During this stage, you should water your plants every other day if it does not rain much in your place. If it rains a lot in one week, you might not need to water at all.

When it comes to nutrients, you should provide nitrogen, phosphorus and potassium (NPK). The ratio between the three macronutrients should be 10-5-7. Add some micronutrients such as zinc, molybdenum, magnesium and iron as well. You can buy all of these from your preferred gardening stores.

As for the sunlight, you cannot do much about it. However, if there are trees in your yard that tend to over your marijuana plants, you should trim the branches of the said trees.

Pre-flowering Phase

The phase between the vegetative and flowering stages is also known as the stretch. This one only takes 10 to 14 days, though. (The vegetative and flowering phases take a month or more.) In this stage, you should gradually increase the water supply and nutrients you give to your marijuana plants. As to the nutrients, you should adjust the ratio of NPK to 5-10-7 or 5-50-17.

In this phase, you have to do the elimination for your male marijuana plants. Do not wait until the 14th day before you proceed with this task. Male marijuana plants tend to mature faster than their female counterparts do so you should act as soon as possible.

Remember to look at the appearance of the buds. Male buds tend to resemble small balls while female buds have hairs.

Flowering Phase

This stage may take 6 to 22 weeks. This is the stage where you can finally see the possible quality and quantity of your harvest. If you are using chemical fertilizers, you have to lessen the supply during the flowering stage to prevent the flowers from tasting and smelling like chemicals. Stop supplying nutrients altogether on the last two weeks. In this phase, the plant will stop growing but it will focus more on producing flowers.

Common Plant Problems and Their Solutions

As a first-time grower, you are likely to make mistakes and it might take a toll on the health of your marijuana plants. When they reach the vegetative phase, many of their health problems may manifest. Below are some signs of common plant problems that many beginners tend to experience with their outdoor marijuana plants.

- Drooping leaves – This is a sign of overwatering. In many instances, the foliage remains green and lean, but it is drooping down from the excessive amounts of water they get. The solution here is quite easy. You have just to lessen the amounts you provide but if it is quite rainy in your place and your plants are on the ground, you might want to put some cover to the soil. Improve drainage as well. Make sure that no standing water is near your plants.

- Limping leaves – This is a sign of under-watering. You have to boost up the amounts of water you provide. Aside from that, get rid of plants or grasses that might be competing with your marijuana plants for water.

- Cupping leaves – This is a sign of heat stress. In this problem, the tips of the leaves are pointed up while the sides are curled up in response to too much heat. In the flowering stage, aside from cupping leaves, extensive growth at the top of the flowers is another sign that the plants are getting too much heat. You may help cool them down by adding some water. Also, you might need to provide some shade to stop the heat from affecting the flowers of your marijuana plants.

- Clawing leaves with brown spots – This is a sign of wind burn. The brown spots are actually burns from strong winds that your plants had to withstand outdoors. Help them by setting up a better fence to lessen the impact of strong winds to the plants.

- Brown spots on lower and middle parts of the leaves – sign of pH fluctuations. The remedy herein is to add compost to your plants. It pays to have your own compost nearby.

Your marijuana may encounter many other plant problems. You can spot these problems on their leaves. They might manifest as brown spots, burnt margins or tips, and yellowish foliage. Always be on the lookout because these problems are going to lessen the potency and quantity of your yield. Also, be mindful of the nutrients you provide. The quantity may be the cause for the plant problems. Adjust the amount you provide accordingly.

Pest Control

Pest control may involve the use of organic solutions, chemical solutions or a combination of both. You can set up fence to fend off the larger pests but for bugs, the battle is harder. Chemical solutions are the fastest of the three. However, too much from these may cause the bugs to develop resistance. You will end up using more, spending more and polluting your soil. It may affect your yield as well. Organic solutions may not be effective but at least they are safe. These are also less expensive. Between the two, organic solutions are better in the long run, unless the pest infestation is severe. For terrible pest infestation, a combination of the two is the most efficient.

Detection is the first step in pest control. This is another reason for you to inspect your plants regularly. Aside from the top sides of the foliage, check the undersides of the leaves and stems, too. Blisters, bites, glossy leaves and webs are some of the signs of insect infestations. Thrips, whiteflies, beetles, mealybugs, leaf miners, aphids, spider mites, snails and slugs are some of the pests that are likely to feast on your marijuana plants.

Organisms

One organic solution is to use your own hands in removing visible pests. Just wear protective gloves for this. Picking snails and slugs should not be a problem.

You may also seek the help of other organisms. You can actually fight off insects with the help of other insects such as lacewings, praying mantises, and ladybugs. These helpful bugs are now being bred commercially to help growers ward off pests organically. Aside from the said bugs, you may also recruit turtles, lizards or birds. You have to leave some food to attract them to your garden though. Be careful when using this method if you only have a small garden as the help you sought might end up becoming pests in the end if they do not have many pests to feast on. You should only consider these if you already have plants that are around two feet tall. If they are still shorter than that, the helpful animals you are introducing may hurt them during their vegetative phase.

Pesticides

Right now, there are organic and chemical pesticides available in many gardening stores and nurseries. As much as possible, you should go with the organic ones as they are made specifically with a plant's natural pest control mechanism in mind. Of all organic pesticides out there, the most sought after is pyrethrum. The downside with all organic pesticides is that, even though they are supposed to be green solutions, they can actually kill even the beneficial animals that are around the area or the animals you introduced. Keep in mind that you are not supposed to use them in the last few weeks of flowering.

The pests may be indicative of other problems in your plants or garden. There may be pH fluctuations, the soil may not be draining well or your plants may not be cleansed properly. Treat these problems along with the pest infestation.

Prevention

The best solution against pests is always prevention. Before you plant, clean your yard well and look for possible pest infestation in your existing plant. You may also apply seaweed extract on the roots of your marijuana plants while they are still on their vegetative phase.

Homemade Remedies

One low-cost preventive solution is that you bath your plants with mild soap and water. To do this, get a gallon of water of water and mix two tablespoons of mild liquid soap. Put your solution in a spray bottle and spritz it evenly on the entire plant. Wait for two minutes before you rinse it off. It is important to get rid of the solution as the soap may damage the plants when left for too long.

You may also mix minced garlic and water. Spraying this mixture can keep beetle and other bugs away from your plants. Just like the soap and water solution, you should wash off the garlic and water mixture as they might cause damage to the plants. The downside with garlic is that the smell might also affect you. Wear a facemask as you spray.

Some growers use alcohol along with the water and soap solution. This can repel snails and slugs in your garden but too much of the alcohol may negatively affect the resin production in your plants. This might also affect the quantity and quality of yield.

You may find other homemade recipes for pest prevention online. Be careful though and make sure to follow the guidelines.

Companion Planting

Unleash the gardener in you by employing companion planting for pest prevention. Onions, cabbages, geraniums, mints and other plants that have a strong smell are good companions for your marijuana plants. Their strong smell is partly because of the chemicals they have that are toxic to some pests. The smell does not only repel the pests from the odorous plants but to the area where they are planted as well.

Aside from pest prevention, this planting technique is beneficial for providing an additional camouflage for your marijuana plants. The downside herein, apart from the possibility that you might have no idea how to plant them, is that they might compete with your marijuana plants for water and nutrients. To prevent this from happening, make sure there is enough water for both the marijuana plants along with their companion plants.

Outdoor marijuana cultivation will make you fall in love with nature. In a few months, you are going to thank it for helping you grow your marijuana plants and providing you with a bountiful yield. The best thing you can do to pay nature back is to use organic farming methods.

Chapter 6: Indoor Cultivation

Indoor marijuana cultivation is an ideal option if you are living in an apartment or condominium, or if you do not have enough space in your yard. If that is what the law in your area says, then you have no other option but to grow your marijuana indoors. It must have a lock if you are living with minors and pets or if you just want to prevent visitors from intruding your plants as they grow quietly.

Growing marijuana indoors may not be the natural and traditional way but it still has advantages on its own. In this method, you can provide better security for your plants against human intrusion, strong wind, heavy rains, and wild animals. This also allows you to control many aspects of the cultivation like water and light supply. With such control, you may be able to influence your plants to flower sooner than their outdoor counterparts may. You can effectively get rid of male plants and prevent the possibility of pollination as well. Outdoors, you may not be able to do the job perfectly due to the possibility of wind carrying pollens from male plants in your area. It is hygienic to cultivate marijuana plants indoor as well. The cleanliness and your control make indoor marijuana cultivation a more suitable option than outdoors for growers who are after the medical benefits of the plants.

However, indoor marijuana cultivation tends to be more expensive than doing it outdoors. You have to prepare for the costs even if you are just planning to raise only a handful of plants in pots. Set aside a budget for utility bills since you will be using electricity and water a lot. Once you have created a spending plan, it is time to start working on your indoor garden or grow room.

Garden Preparation

Unlike outdoor cultivation, you do not have to mind the season to kick off your indoor marijuana cultivation. You are not going to depend too much on the sunlight and rainwater anyway. Decide the number of plants early on to determine the size of your grow room.

Room Preparation

Clear out the room you will be using. Take out all of the unnecessary furniture. Get rid of curtains, clothes, carpet or any other item where mold may grow.

There should be total darkness during the flowering phase to avoid disrupting the plants. Therefore, the room where you want to place them should have no holes where lights may enter. It is important that you set up a room even if you are planning to place your plants near a windowsill during the vegetative phase. Any lights that unintentionally enter the room may confuse your marijuana plants and trigger their hermaphroditism during the flowering phase. They will have seeded flowers. Overall, the quantity and quality of your yield will be affected.

Cover windows or any holes with tough materials. Fabric and paper are not ideal because they might get easily torn and punctured. Paper does not go well with water spills as well. Fabric may become breeding ground for mold. You can seal holes with opaque reflective tape.

There should be drainage as well. Standing water can affect the pH level of your soil when left for a long time. It may attract pests as well.

The grow room should have an area of 1 to 2 square meters. The distance between the lamps and plants matter, too. Make sure the lights and your plants are at least 50 centimeters away from each other.

Grow boxes and grow tents are also worth considering. Each one can hold at least 8 plants. Some can even hold up to 200 plants. Decide the number of plants you are about to cultivate then choose the appropriate grow box or grow tent if you do not want to dedicate an entire room for growing them.

A grow box or grow tent is a great space- and time-saver. It often comes with its own lights and exhaust system. They are also water-proof. You only need to do a few things to make them ideal for your indoor marijuana cultivation. The only downside is its price. However, you may reuse it multiple times as long as you are taking good care of it. It is usable for hydroponic cultivation as well. The best thing about it is that it does not require excessive modifications in your home.

Container

You should buy separate pots for the seedlings and vegetative phases. The right size of the pots depends on the expected height of marijuana plants. For 1- to 2-foot plants, 3 to 5 gallon pots or containers are the most suitable. For 3-foot plants, 5 to 7 gallon pots or containers are the most appropriate while for those up to 4-foot and beyond, 6 to 8 gallon pots or containers are the best options. You should also buy saucers or trays that will catch runoff water.

Growing medium

Get organic soil as growing medium. You may also opt for coco-, peat-, or sphagnum-based mediums. You should make sure that your growing medium is sterilized. Do not just get random soil from public places as they might have eggs from pests.

Artificial Lighting

Photoperiod is an important aspect of marijuana cultivation. Photoperiod refers to the time when the plants receive light. With indoor cultivation, you can only fulfill this need artificially.

Even if you are placing your plants beside the windowsill, it is still important to provide them with a more stable source of light. For marijuana grown in a closet or small area, lights with low wattages (250-400 watts) will suffice. You may even opt for regular fluorescents for such.

For marijuana cultivated in a more spacious room, lights with high wattages (600-1000 watts) are recommended. Metal Halide (MH) and High-Pressure Sodium (HPS) bulbs and ballasts are the ideal lighting equipment for these.

When you shop for lights, always try to find if there are LED lights available. These ones tend not to heat as much as traditional lights.

LED lights costs more upfront but they are energy efficient and cost less in the long run. In contrast, HPS and ML are less expensive but their usage tends to cost more. LED lights also have built-in fan while HPS and ML requires ballasts that allows cooling. You are going to need an outlet timer as well because the plants require specific time frames for their photoperiod.

Improve light reflection in your grow room to use the light more efficiently. For small rooms, emergency blankets are good options because they can reflect up to 70% of light. These are available in camping stores. White paint and aluminized mylar are more suitable and more efficient in reflecting light for sizable grow rooms. White paint is inexpensive and easy to apply. It can reflect up to 85% of light. Another plus point is its ease of maintenance. Mylar is the most efficient at 97% light reflection but it is also the most expensive. Never use aluminum foil. They do not reflect light well. Aside from that, it is a fire hazard and hard to attach.

Ventilation

There should be fans with ducts providing air for the lights and dragging the warmth from the said lights out of the grow room. This helps in temperature control too. This helps tone down the smell from marijuana as well.

When shopping for fans, always keep in mind the level of noise for their operation and go for something with high CFM rating. Inline fans are worth considering because they are easy to attach to existing ducts.

Temperature

The ideal temperature range of the grow room is 24 to 30 degrees Celsius. Buy and install glass casing to prevent the warmth from the lights from burning your plants. For LED lights, you do not need such glass casing at all. Install a thermometer to help you manage temperature levels.

Smell

Get rid of the stale odor with the help of a carbon filter. Attach the carbon filter into your exhaust fan. You may also use ozone generators.

Humidity

Buy a humidifier, dehumidifier and humidity meter for your grow room. The different growth phases of the marijuana plants require different humidity levels. This help in managing possible mold infestation as well.

Nutrients

Use sea kelp, bat guano and other organic nutrients. You may purchase these separately or you can buy them along with the organic soil you buy. Avoid artificial nutrients due to their high salt content.

The nutrients for indoor marijuana cultivation are the same as the ones for the outdoors. Buy packs of the macro- and micronutrients from nearby gardening stores. Refer to the packaging to know the right amount for each phase and the preparation.

Water

Tap water is already a good option for your plants. However, you want to know first the pH level of the water. It should be within the range 5.8 to 7. You may boost the pH level of your water by adding lime slices or wood ash. You may also buy a pre-mixed solution. Add pH-lowering solution if the pH level is too high.

Once you are done preparing these things, you may now proceed to seed selection. Go for strains that are shorter than the traditional cannabis plants.

Plant Care and Training

Plant care for indoor marijuana plants is different because training is not optional but it is necessary. Training entails controlling the growth of the plants by modifying them. This is to prevent their stems and leaves from going all over the room. This is to ensure shorter growth as well as denser canopy.

Seedling Phase

In this phase, the plants need 18 to 24 hours of light. Lamps with lower intensity are ideal for the seedling phase. Supply the needed nutrients in the water. Start small then gradually increase as your plants get bigger. The humidity should be 70% to 80%. Use a humidifier to achieve such humidity levels.

Vegetative Phase

During this phase, you may need to transfer your plants to bigger pots. If the plants remain in their small pot for a long time, their roots may not be able to grow properly. This also affects the growth of the entire plants. To transfer, hold the entire soil along with the roots.

Allow the plants to vegetate before inducing them to flower. In this phase, indoor marijuana plants require at least 16 hours of light. If you want to speed up the vegetative phase, you may give your plants 18 to 20 hours of light.

Reduce humidity level in this phase, too. It should be around 50% to 70%. You can achieve this range by using a dehumidifier. You may also opt to boost the rate of exhaust fan.

Employ training during the vegetative phase when the plants grow twice or thrice than their original height. Topping and pinching are common training methods. These are simple and do not require any special equipment.

In topping, you cut the main stem to your preferred plant height. While the main stem heals, other stems of the plants develop faster than usual. If the other stems grow to undesired height, you may employ topping again. However, do not apply this training method more than three times as it may lower down the quality and quantity of yield.

Pinching is similar to topping but instead of cutting, you just need to pinch the main stem. The lower stems develop more rapidly while the main stem heals. The plants may still grow taller as the main stem may still develop after it gets healed.

Low stress training (LSTing) is another way to train your marijuana plants. In this method, you are going to bend and tie the stems of your plants. You need to employ topping first though . A few weeks after, do the bending and tying of stems. This training is also applicable to outdoor marijuana plants if they are likely to grow beyond 5 feet.

Advanced training technique includes Screen of Green (SCROG). This requires a screen in the form of chicken wire. This screen is placed at the top of the plants to prevent the stems from growing beyond it. This requires proper timing. Do not induce flowering until 70% to 80% of the screen is full. If the screen is too full, it may become crowded and the buds may not develop into flowers properly. If you induce flowering while there is still much space in your screen, you will end up with wasted space.

Pre-flowering Phase

When your marijuana plants have grown into your preferred height, it is time to induce them to flower. For the pre-flowering phase, you have to do the cycle of 12-hour light and 12-hour darkness. During this phase, you have to get rid of male marijuana plants.

Flowering Phase

The strongest lights are needed in this phase. If using LED lights, add more on this stage but make sure to shut them down every 12 hours and let them on for 12 hours. An outlet timer can help you sustain this cycle more efficiently. Auto-flowering plants will not need this cycle. You can keep in the room where others are still in their seedling or vegetative phase. Further lower the humidity level in this phase to keep diseases at bay. The ideal humidity level for the flowering phase ranges from 40% to 50%.

Hydroponics

With indoor cultivation, you may also apply hydroponics after you learn the basics. This technique entails replacing the traditional soil medium with water-soluble fertilizer. It helps you produce more flowers in a shorter period of time but there is a catch: setting up and operating a hydroponic system is a challenging and costly endeavor. This is worth considering if you have plans of selling your produce afterwards. The following are six options you can choose from for a hydroponic system:

- Aeroponic System – this is the most effective but the most expensive. This involves a mist that sprays nutrients to the roots of marijuana plants, and a dark sealed box where the roots are kept hanging. Compared to other growing mediums, this means the plants can get more oxygen. The problem with this is that when there is power interruption, the mist will stop working and your plants will die.

- Deep Water Culture – this is relatively easy to maintain when compared to other hydroponic systems. The roots of the marijuana plants are in oxygenated nutrient solution. The problem with this, though, is that the plants may also die when there is power interruption and the system stops working. Hydroton clay pebbles and Rockwool are possible growing mediums for this hydroponic system.

- Nutrient Film – this is also effective in achieving greater yield but this is meant for experienced growers. This requires expertise in managing the tilted tray, the main feature of this hydroponic system. Multiple marijuana plants are put in the said tray. The nutrients are flown down in the said tray and pumped back afterwards.

- Ebb and Flow – this has a relatively simple mechanism. This involves plant containers and a nutrient reservoir. Coco peat and Rockwool are the growing mediums meant for this hydroponic system. With an ebb and flow system, the nutrient reservoir provides a nutrient-rich solution to the containers of your plants on certain periods. The solution slowly goes back to the reservoir, then the reservoir supplies the solution again.

- Top Feed/Drip Feed – this works similarly to ebb and flow system. The difference is that the nutrients are dripped, not flown, to the roots. The nutrients get drawn back to the nutrient reservoir. Appropriate growing mediums for this are Rockwool, coco peat and hydroton clay pebbles.

- Passive Wick System – this is the most commonly used of all types of hydroponic systems. Coco peat, peat moss and vermiculate are the three ideal growing mediums for this hydroponic system. The plants just sit in their growing mediums then the wick draws up nutrients from the solution below them.

Common Plant Problems and Their Solutions

Indoor marijuana plants are not immune to problems. Aside from those mentioned for the outdoor plants, you should also look for the following signs of plant problems common to marijuana plants grown indoors.

- Yellowish leaves with burnt tips – sign of light burn. Your indoor marijuana plants might be too close to the grow lights. Move the lights further or if it is fixed in place, move your pots lower or further away

- Patches of white powder in the leaves – sign of mildew. The patches of white are actually white powdery mildew or simply known as WPM. This can be remedied immediately. It is easy but do not underestimate this as it might trigger rotting buds later on. Get rid of them as soon as possible by washing them with a homemade remedy. You may mix 4 teaspoons of Neem Oil in one gallon of water. You may also substitute this mixture with milk and water (1:9 ratio) or baking soda and water (2 tablespoons to one gallon).

- Rotting buds – sign of mold growth inside. There is nothing much you can do to save the affected buds. However, you can prevent the other buds from getting affected. Cut the rotten buds immediately. Trim down some leaves as well, especially those that are near the rotten buds. The mold is a sign of high humidity in your grow room so improve ventilation and use a dehumidifier to further lower the humidity levels.

Pest Control

You should act fast when it comes to pest control for indoor marijuana plants. You may go with organic pesticides or get rid of the pests manually. You do not need to build a fence. You do not need to buy helpful bugs as well as they might dwell inside your home.

Pest Prevention

You are not likely to get slugs, snails or other bugs in your indoor marijuana grow room. As long as you keep the room clean, there should not be much pest infestation. You should maintain a tidy home too. Seal random holes and repair leaks to prevent pests such as rats and snakes from coming in. They might not be interested with your plants but they might impair vital components of your grow room. Keep your tools sterilized as well.

Indoor marijuana cultivation is very intricate. However, it will be a rewarding one. It is like bringing nature closer to your home.

Chapter 7: Harvesting

After months of waiting and caring for your plants, it is time to reap the flowers that you waited for so long. For some, this stage in cultivation is the most fulfilling part. It may even give a more rewarding feeling than the consumption. The great feeling comes from the idea that you are done with the toughest parts of the cultivation process.

There are three major considerations for the harvesting stage and these are: timing, drying and curing. This will help determine the taste of your buds later on.

Timing

This aspect is important because if you do it too early, the beneficial components of the produce may be too low or too insignificant. If you are too late, the said components may degrade. For the timing, do not just rely on the rough estimate from your seed supplier.

To know the proper timing, you have to evaluate the leaves and flowers of your marijuana plants. The tips of most leaves are going to turn yellow as they near maturity. You may remove these leaves to allow flowers below to receive light.

You should inspect the trichomes or the crystal-like parts in the flowers as well. You are going to need magnifying glass for this step. The shape of a trichome is likened to mushroom up close. They look like dews due to their colorless appearance. However, they will turn amber when they are nearing maturity. You may harvest during the time they turn amber or when they appear cloudy.

You may also assess the pistils or the white hairs in your flowers. Do not harvest when there are still new hairs growing. When there is no more new growth, wait until they turn dark. You may start harvesting when 50% to 90% of the hairs have darkened.

To harvest, get a large knife and pruners. Use the pruners to get rid of the large marijuana leaves. Leave the small ones because they protect the trichomes. Use the knife to cut each branch. Handle each branch with care to avoid wasting the trichomes.

Drying

Drying takes a few days to two weeks. You may set up a drying box or buy a readymade drying cabinet. It should have a fan but it should not be directed to the marijuana flowers. The flowers are regarded as dried when the stems seem to crack easily instead of bending. You may already roll the flowers and smoke them but if you want a better-tasting joint, proceed to curing.

Curing

Have mason jars for this stage. Use small scissors to further remove some of the remaining leaves. You may place the cuttings in a separate container so you may use them for cooking later on. Separate the flower buds from the stems individually. Fill each mason jar with flower buds up to 75%.

Curing is important because it gets rid the grassy smell and taste of the plant. For the first two weeks, open the jars twice a day for 15 minutes. This will help remove the remaining moisture. You may only open it once a week after that. In the 4th week, you may open it once a month. You may continue doing this until the 6th month. After that, keep your cured marijuana in a jar for longer storage.

You may trade your stored marijuana. You may cook using them. You may use them for smoking. Best of all, enjoy the health benefits from your homegrown remedy.

Conclusion

Thank you again for purchasing this book!

I hope this book was able to help you to grow marijuana successfully, be it outdoors or indoors. Hopefully, it was able to guide in the entire process—from selecting the best seeds to harvesting the fruits of your labor. Most of all, I wish your yield is high in terms of quality and quantity.

The next step is to enjoy your produce. Share your newfound knowledge to friends who may also be interested with taking their love to marijuana to another level.

Thank you and good luck!

CBD Hemp Oil

Everything You Need to Know About
CBD Hemp Oil

Introduction

History shows that one of the first plants utilized as usable fiber was the industrial hemp or hemp. This versatile, durable and naturally-soft fiber plant was refined into clothing, paper, textiles, oil, food, biofuel, medicine, rope, animal feeds, insulation, paint and biodegradable plastics.

But did you know that, hemp was also used as money or legal tender in America for more than 200 years? People during those times could pay taxes with hemp. It was so valuable in England and America that when farmers failed to grow cannabis in their fields, they were sent to jail or penalized.

Sadly, the golden years of hemp eventually ended. Many nations, such as the United States of America, regulated the production and use of hemp. In 1937, the cultivation and commercial sale of cannabis varieties was strictly monitored by virtue of *Marijuana Tax Act*. Forty-seven years after, all types of cannabis were classified as a Schedule I drug under Controlled Substances Act of 1970. Since hemp was part of this plant species, growing it inside United States became a taboo.

For many years, lawmakers and farmers fought to decriminalize the cultivation of hemp in the U.S. Finally, hope became apparent when the US Farm Bill of 2014 allowed different states that passed their industrial hemp legislation to cultivate the plant for research and development purposes. These states included the following: Colorado, Oregon and Kentucky, all three of which were already conducting pilot projects of growing hemp. Many states followed and soon enough, American farmers were reacquainting themselves with hemp's industrial benefits after a very long period of strict prohibition.

The possible repeal of prohibition and regulation resulted to the passage of The Industrial Hemp Farming Act of 2015. If it passed into law, this will end the federal restrictions to grow industrial hemp in U.S., and remove it under Schedule I classification of controlled substance. To date, hemp under this classification is considered a dangerous drug, no different from ecstasy, heroin and LSD.

Chapter 1: Getting to Know Hemp

Hemp is considered as a highly-sustainable and renewable resource which can easily thrive in almost any climate and soil conditions across the world. "Industrial hemp" is referred to as plant Cannabis sativa L. with delta-9 tetrahydrocannabinol (THC) concentration of 0.3% on dry-weight basis. It is based on Section 7606 of Agricultural Appropriations Act of 2014.

Over 30 countries produce different varieties of industrial hemp. In 2011, China became the top producer and world supplier of hemp. Chile and the European Union followed closely as second and third respectively. The thriving potential of hemp market attracted Canada to produce more. In 2013, the nation managed to reach an annual crop high of 66,700 acres.

The Hemp Industries Association (HIA) has estimated an average total retail value of $620 million for clothing, building materials, food products, CBD oil and other hemp-containing products.

It was once the top major crop of U.S. but because it is deemed illegal, raw material has to be imported from other countries. United States is one of the largest importers of industrial hemp. It is not illegal for the country to import raw products of hemp inside the country. Hemp Industry Association reported that every year, U.S. importation of hemp reached about $500 million.

The Re-emergence of Hemp Industry

When CNN featured, back in in 2013, a documentary entitled "Charlotte's Web cannabis", an increased demand of CBD producing hemp spread across the US. In Kentucky, a legislation to promote hemp farming as one of major development program of the state was passed to assist tobacco farmers who are suffering from drastic absence of market for their crops. The state of Kentucky strongly lobbied to make hemp production legal and won.

As of 2017, 31 states in United States were able to legalize hemp production. This includes the states of: Colorado, California, Indiana, Montana, Maine, North Dakota, North Carolina, Oregon, South Carolina, Tennessee, Vermont and West Virginia.

Other states also passed legislations which authorized pilot studies or researches to grow industrial hemp plants. These include Utah, Nebraska, Kentucky, Illinois, Hawaii, Delaware and Connecticut.

Resolutions that support revisions of federal rules and regulations for commercial production of hemp were later adopted by the National Conference of State Legislatures and the National Association of State Departments of Agriculture.

In Utah, people who possess CBD supplements are exempted from penalties imposed under Controlled Substances Act if they have a Hemp Extract Registration Card which is signed by an authorized neurologist. The neurologist must indicate in the card that the person is showing symptoms of intractable epilepsy or is in need of the substance for health reasons. A regular submission of evaluation data to the Utah Department of Health is another task that the neurologist needs to comply. The user must also obtain a certificate of extract analysis from hemp's product seller.

In New Zealand, anyone who wants to use CBD hemp products would have to seek the approval of Health Ministry. Cannabidiol remains as a class B1 controlled drug under Misuse of Drugs Act and a prescription drug under Medicines Act. Before the changes in the rules, the sole way to get prescription was to get the Minister of Health's personal approval. At present, doctors can prescribe CBD to patients who are in dire need of its benefits.

In Canada, CBD is a Schedule II drug and is only obtainable with prescription.

In Europe, CBD is listed in both EU Cosmetics Ingredient Database and EU Novel Food Catalogue. However, crude extracts of hemp are not listed-- only synthetic CBD. A position paper for regulatory framework was issued by the European Industrial Hemp Association. At present, there are hemp varieties that are grown legally in the western part of Europe. One of them is "Fedora 17", a cannabis plant with 1%

cannabidiol (CBD) and 0.1% THC.

In Sweden, CBD is not classified. One product that contains CBD and THC, called Sativex, is available upon prescription. It brings relief for illnesses such as severe spasticity, a symptom of Multiple Sclerosis.

In the United Kingdom, people with Multiple Sclerosis can avail, upon prescription, a CDB spray which is laden with delta-9-THC. On December 31, 2016, CBD products with the purpose of addressing medical conditions were classified as medicines by the Medicines and Healthcare products Regulatory Agency (MHRA). However, a regulatory approval must first be secured for medical claims before they can be commercially available for users.

In Switzerland, CBD products are legally sold in the country and not subjected to Swiss Narcotics Act. However, the product must contain less than 1% THC since THC is still illegal there.

Varieties of Hemp

Hemp has many varieties. Each of them offers unique characteristics and nutritional values to people using them. The most-sought after variety which is used to manufacture CBD hemp oil has very high concentration content.

Fiber and oilseed varieties of Cannabis are known as industrial hemp. These varieties do not contain the addictive component that is prohibited in many countries.

Different varieties of Cannabis grow at different density conditions. They are also harvested at different periods.

Industrial hemp varieties seeding rate differ per acre. The recommended seeding rate to produce hemp fiber is 60 pounds per acre (30-35 plants for every square foot). Finola is seeded at 30 pounds per acre while Crag , USO 31 and USO 14 are seeded at 20 pounds per acre

Cultivation of Cannabis Varieties across the World

The USDA used an extensive range of hemp varieties in their breeding program during the time of Lyster H. Dewey until his retirement in 1930s. They named the varieties as Simple Leaf, Michigan Early and Minnesota No. 8. Other varieties which they bred but became extinct were Chington, Ferramington, Kymington, Tochimington and Chinamington.

At present, there are many cultivars or varieties of hemp in different seed banks across the world.

The European Union (EU) certified 26 hemp varieties to be cultivated. All these varieties contain low to almost zero levels of tetrahydrocannabinol (THC). The most sought-after variety of industrial hemp produces about 1-5% of pure botanical cannabidiol (CBD) oil.

In Canada, the common varieties which are approved by Health Canada List of Approved Cultivars:

- USO 14

- Finola (formerly called FIN 314)

- Crag

- USO 31

- Alyssa

- Felina 34

These hemp varieties are part of the 2007 List of Approved Cultivars based on Organization for Economic Co-operation and Development (OECD). The OECD is an economic development organization founded in 1961 with main office in Paris, France. One of the 30 members is the United States.

The largest Cannabis collection in the world is the "germplasm" which is now preserved at N.I.Vavilov Research Institute of Plant Industry (VIR). The VIR collection before World War II numbered at about 1400 accessions but today there are only 491 remaining.

Finland's Dr. J.C. Callaway bred the oilseed cultivar Finola with VIR germplasm and became a success. Now, it is grown in various northern countries. Finola is known as the earliest maturing hemp variety and can produce a great amount of seeds. It contains optimum amounts of omega-3 and omega -6 fatty acids. Research shows that compared to other oilseed varieties, Finola has higher amount of SDA and GLA fatty acids.

2017 List of Approved Cannabis sativa L. Industrial Hemp Cultivars

The following hemp varieties are licensed for 2017 commercial cultivation pursuant to Industrial Hemp Regulations Subsection 39 (1). The list shows the countries where they are cultivated.

- Alyssa - Canada
- Anka - Canada
- Canda - Canada
- CanMa - Canada
- Carmagnola -Italy
- Carmen - Canada
- CFX-1 - Canada
- CFX-2 -Canada
- Crag - Canada
- CRS-1 -Canada
- CS - Italy

- Delores - Canada

- Deni - Canada

- ESTA-1 - Canada

- Fasamo - Germany

- Fedrina 74 - France

- Felina 34 - France

- Ferimon - France

- Fibranova - Italy

- Fibriko - Hungary

- Fibrimon 24 -France

- Fibrimon 56 -France

- FINOLA - Canada (Finland)

- Georgina - Canada

- GranMa - Canada

- Grandi - Canada

- Joey - Canada

- Judy - Canada

- Jutta - Canada

- Katani - Canada

- Kompolti - Hungary

- Kompolti Hibrid TC - Hungary

- Kompolti Sargaszaru - Hungary

- Lovrin 110 - Romania

- Petera - Canada

- Picolo - Canada

- Silesia - Canada

- UC-RGM - Canada

- Uniko B - Hungary

- USO 14 - Canada (Ukraine)

- USO 31 - Canada (Ukraine)

- Victoria - Canada

- X-59 (Hemp Nut) - Canada

- Yvonne - Canada

- Zolotonosha 11 - Canada (Ukraine)

- Zolotonosha 15 - Canada (Ukraine)

All the seeds used to produce industrial hemp in Canada are required to be of pedigreed status or certified based on Subsection 14 (3) of Industrial Hemp Regulations (IHR). Farmers with saved seeds must be Certified-seeds before they are allowed to be planted. They must request for inspection and need official seed tags as evidence that they comply with the regulations.

The regulation also restricts direct importation of the above-mentioned seeds if they are not recognized by Seed Certification Schemes (SCS), of which Canada is an active member. The country is also a member of two other schemes – the Association of Official Seed Certifying Agencies (AOSCA) and Organization for Economic Cooperation and Development (OECD).

Countries Producing Industrial Hemp

France is now the leading producer of hemp in the world. It produces over 70% of the total global output. The second in rank is China which provides a quarter of the world production. Other nations which contribute to the overall hemp output in the market are Europe, North Korea and Chile.

Industrial hemp are now grown and supplied by more than 30 countries across the world including Austria, Australia, Chile, Canada, China, Denmark, Egypt, Finland, Great Britain, Greece, Germany, Hungary, Italy, India, Japan, Korea, New Zealand, Netherlands, Portugal, Poland, Russia, Romania, Spain, Slovenia, Switzerland, Sweden, Turkey, Thailand and Ukraine.

Companies in United Kingdom, United States, Canada and Germany are among the many that process hemp seeds into a number of other commodities including: cosmetics, food products and textile-grade fibers. British production targets horses' beddings. Germany and United Kingdom stopped commercial production for a long time then resumed in 1990s.

Hemp was believed to be one of the earliest grown plants and is still thriving at present. In 8000 BC, archeologists discovered a site in Japan's Oki Islands that contained cannabis of the Achenes variety. But this isn't the first and only known use of the plant in ancient history.

There's plenty of evidence that even the earliest civilizations made use of the plant for many different reasons—some, not too different from how we use it today.

The beneficial uses of hemp can be dated back to Neolithic Age, where fiber imprints have been found in China's Yangshao pottery culture. Hemp was mainly utilized by the ancient Chinese to make ropes, clothes, shoes and paper. The Greek historian Herodotus, in 480 BC, wrote that Scythia inhabitants used to inhale hemp-seed smoke during their ritual rites and for recreation.

Chapter 2: Hemp versus Marijuana

Both hemp and marijuana come from the Cannabis sativa L. specie. The term cannabis is oftentimes associated with the more recreational use of the plant, often smoked by people who are looking to get "high". The mislabeling of marijuana as a recreational yet dangerous drug has significant affected the marketing of industrial hemp, with many people thinking that these two things are the same.

THEY ARE NOT.

It is unfortunate that they are mistakenly regarded as similar because of their tetrahydrocannabinol (THC) content. However, the quantity of THC in hemp is only about .3 to 1.5% THC, much less when compared to the 20% THC content of marijuana.

Hemp is not marijuana, and marijuana is not hemp. They are also genetically different. Each has its distinct uses and chemical components.

Even their cultivation methods are not the same. The fruits and blooms of hemp produces strong fibers and seeds. On the other hand, Marijuana flowers and buds are often used to produce psychoactive effects.

Hemp also contains a high-amount of concentrated

cannabidiol or CBD which acts as a neutralizer of psychoactive effects that its THC bring. It does not give the same psychoactive sensation that marijuana does simply because the small amount of THC in it is processed immediately by the body.

The hemp plant is can be easily grown outdoors to produce maximum yields and size. It does not require pesticides or a high-amount of water to thrive. As it grows, it can actually help with detoxifying the soil, removes any traces of carbon dioxide in the air and prevents soil erosion problem.

Marijuana on the other hand needs grow-room conditions with a sustained oxygen level, CO_2, humidity, temperature and stable light in order to achieve the optimum level of THC content. It is far more delicate than hemp as well.

- Industrial hemp is categorized as agricultural crop. Marijuana and other drug variety of Cannabis plant is horticultural crop.

- Drug varieties are planted without spacing and pruning while oilseed/fiber varieties are planted like pulp wood trees.

- Drug varieties which are grown as drug crops give you drugs. Oilseed varieties grown as fiber crops give oilseed. Fiber varieties grown as fiber crops give fibers.

- When different varieties are grown with dual purpose, this basically doubles your harvest and you can maximize the benefit of the plant itself. If you grow oilseed and fiber varieties as dual purpose crop, they yield fiber and oilseed. If you grow oilseed and fiber varieties as drug crop, they would not produce drugs.

- Hemp seeding rates are measurable by pounds per acre. Drug-varieties seeds are measured by ounces per acre.

- Oilseed varieties seeding rates are about 20-30 pounds per acre. Fiber varieties are rates are 40-90 pounds per acre. Cannabis drug varieties seeding rates are at 18-48 ounces per acre.

Marijuana and other drug-type varieties of Cannabis utilizes the flowers of female plants. Males are cut down or pulled out because they do not yield the same effects.

Industrial hemp varieties grow up to about 16 feet high. They have strong, long stalks with very few branches. They can be bred to produce maximum amount of seed and fiber. They are grown in 100-300 plants per square yard high densities.

Some varieties are typically shorter, bred to produce maximum branching, and not allowed to seed. They are grown densely to yield more drug-producing leaves and flowers.

Chapter 3: Benefits and Side Effects of CBD

CBD or cannabidiol is the main component found in the industrial hemp variety of cannabis. It has a molecular mass of about 314.4636 with formula $C_{21}H_{30}O_2$.

It is one of 113 active cannabis cannabinoids, and is considered a major phytocannabinoid which accounts to about 40% of hemp-extracted components. It does not give the same intoxicating effect of marijuana, but provides anti-psychotic and anti-stress benefits.

Various research and studies done throughout the decades show that cannabinoids or CBD actively interact with the endogenous cannabinoid system (ECS) of the body. This particular body system is complex, but is known to contribute to different biological processes such as appetite, sleeping, relaxation, hormone regulation, immunity, pains and inflammation responses. The interaction of cannabidoid in the endocannabinoid system assists homeostasis or the regulation of balance in the body.

According to scientific studies, the human body has 2 prime receptors of cannabinoids, these are known as CB1 and CB2. They are found within the cells of our body. Imagine million tiny cannabinoid receptor sites in the central nervous system and brain (CB1) while the rest are found in the immune system (CB2). These receptors interact through the neural communication process.

What is interesting to note is that the human body does not simply rely on cannabinoids produced by plants (phytocannabinoids). Mammals, especially humans, are capable of producing natural cannabinoids – the 2-AG and Anandamite. These two natural compounds which help the body control neural communication and mediate various cellular functions.

This vital information clearly showed that endocannabinoid system (ECS) is a very functional and essential regulatory system.

Medical Benefits of CBD

Many people from various parts of the world are starting to turn to the use of CBD to help cure their different health concerns.

Recent studies indicated that CBD contains anti-inflammatory, anti-anxiety and analgesic properties minus THC's psychoactive effects. To help you better understand this, below are the known benefits you can derive from the use of CBD:

CBD is associated with Adenosine receptor site activation. Cannabidoid can trigger the abundant release of glutamate neurotransmitters and dopamine. Glutamate is connected to cognition, memory formation, learning and excitatory signals. Dopamine is popularly known to aid in various processes including motor control, motivation, reward mechanism and cognition.

CBD is also known as pleitropic drug which can effectively pass through various molecular pathways. It also inhibits the potential binding action of different receptors like the G-coupled proteins receptor.

CBD is greatly involved in 5-Ht1A serotonin receptor stimulation which provides anti-depressant effects. This receptor is directly involved with anxiety, appetite, nausea, pain perception and addiction.

CBD inhibits GPR55 signalling which remarkably reduces bone reabsorption, modulating the bone density, blood pressure control and hinders the proliferation of cancer cells.

CBD is utilized as anti-cancer treatment. When peroxisome proliferator activated receptors (PPAR) are fully activated in gamma level, they can induce significant regression of tumors in lung cancer cells. PPAR receptors are usually located on cell nucleus surfaces.

CBD can effectively stop cervical cancer cells from spreading.

It decreases the ability of the tumor or cancer cells to produce energy which eventually weakens them and leads to the cells' natural death.

CBD-induced treatment assists lymphokine-activated killer (LAK) cells to overpower and kill debilitating cancer cells. It kills tumor cells found in colon cancer and leukemia. It decreases glioma cell invasion and growth. It is being studied as potential combination therapy for prostate and breast cancers.

CBD is eyed as potential remedy to treat Alzheimer's disease. The process involves hindering the development of PPAR-gamma amyloid-beta plaque. This molecule is considered the key link to the early stages of this disease.

CBD can benefit diabetics. PPAR receptors regulate insulin sensitivity, lipid uptake, energy homeostasis and metabolic functions. In a controlled experiment using non-obese mice, the onset of diabetes was prevented. Researchers explained that cannabidiol did not have a direct effect on glucose levels, however, it actively blocked splenocytes to produce IL-12, a type of cytokine which plays big role in different autoimmune diseases.

CBD can potentially alleviate the symptoms of epilepsy. It also controls the intensity and frequency of seizures. However, thorough research is still being done to gain more understanding regarding this matter.

CBD can treat neuropsychiatric disorders which are also linked to epilepsy. This includes neuronal injury, psychiatric diseases and neurodegeneration. It can prevent toxicity which affects brain's radical oxygen species (ROS) and neurotransmitter glutamate which effectively prevent the death of brain cells. It can also protect the brain from the danger of ischemia.

CBD can control the development of Prion. Prions are types of proteins in the body which can bring neurogenerative diseases including Mad Cow and Creutzfeldt-Jakob. In 2007, the Journal of Neuroscience published the result of studies documenting the ability of CBD to stop the accumulation and formation of prions.

CBD is a possible cure for schizophrenia. German researchers conducted a controlled study among 42 patients in 2012. They used CBD and Amisulpride, a potent antipsychotic drug used for schizophrenic attacks. Both showed effectiveness, but with significant side effects. However, those who made use of CBD experienced far shorter post-treatment side effects when compared to others. The result of this study was published in Translational Psychiatry.

CBD is a potential treatment for Crohn's Disease. The anti-inflammatory components of cannabis can bring relief for bowel diseases including Crohn's Disease. Studies show that the CBD and THC compounds of cannabis can effectively interact and controls gut functions.

CBD can reduce effects of multiple sclerosis. Using cell culture and controlled animal models, the Cajal Institute scientists used CBD to find its effect to MS. The result showed positive effects. First, it reversed the inflammatory responses of the body. Second, it acted as a strong protection against the effects of the disease.

Other benefits include:

- *Natural Pain Reliever*

  CBD is a natural cure to lower mild to chronic pain. The non-psychoactive compounds it contains are being studied as a potential new treatment to ease chronic pain. Today, it is also utilized to help treat fibromyalgia and multiple sclerosis.

  A 2011 experimental study which used CBD to treat fibromyalgia resulted to a promising result. Half of 56 participants were given CBD while the other half were given traditional anti-inflammatory drugs like corticosteroids and opioid. Those who used CBD induced treatment showed reduced pains and symptoms while those who used traditional cure continued experiencing discomfort.

- *Prevents and Controls Inflammation*

Cannabidiol (CBD) decreases the growth and migration of neutrophils which trigger inflammation in the body. It also reduces B-cells chemokines production of macrophage inflammatory protein-1 alpha (MIP-1 alpha) and macrophage inflammatory protein-1 beta (MIP-1 beta).

This ability of CBD makes it a potential therapeutic agent against various inflammatory disorders and pains.

- *Aids Drug and Smoking Withdrawal Symptoms*

CBD is a potential treatment to assist people who seriously want to quit smoking. A pilot study where smokers were given inhalers with CBD compounds resulted to lesser cravings for nicotine. The participants would simply need to take a puff whenever they feel urge to smoke cigarette. It brought about a 40% drop of their cigarette consumption and eased the symptoms associated with the withdrawal process. The result of this experiment was published in *Addictive Behaviors*.

Another experiment was conducted to discover the CBD effect to those addicted to opioid substances. The positive result was published in *Neurotherapeutics*.

- *Alleviates symptoms of anxiety disorders*

  It can be a potential cure for generalized anxiety disorder (GAD), post-traumatic stress disorder (PTSD), social anxiety, panic disorder and obsessive-compulsive disorder (OCD), as well as mild-to-severe cases of depression. CBD-induced treatment calms the patient and brings stable mental state.

  Cannabinoids receptors in the brain are located in the area which regulates emotional behavior and responses, irritability, stress, fear, moods, sleep and "cravings". This part of the brain is comprised of the periaquenductal gray (PAG) of middle brain, hippocampus, prefrontal cortex, nucleus accumbens and amygdala. With presence of cannabidiol (CBD), the "fight or flight" stress sensation is triggered.

  CBD treatment didn't show adverse effects when used for the above-mentioned disorders, a significant improvement compared to commercially-available medications.

- *Aids in curing insomnia*

  Cannabis is a natural herb which can bring about a more relaxed stated and help people drift into easeful sleep. CBD-heavy strains treatment creates feelings of tiredness, one of its more positive side effects when it comes to insomnia. Unlike sleeping pills, the good thing about the CBD treatment is that it is non-habit forming.

- *Heals Acne*

This is also a potential cure for acne vulgaris. Acne is commonly caused by overworked sebaceous body glands or an inflammation inside the body. CBD treatment lowers sebum production and reduces inflammation. Cannabidiol acts like an anti-inflammatory and sebostatic agent which effectively inhibits lipid synthesis.

In summary, CBD is:

- anticonvulsant – it suppresses seizures

- antiemetic – reduces and alleviates vomiting or nausea

- anti-inflammatory – fights inflammatory issues

- antipsychotic – combats psychosis

- anti-cancer/anti-tumor - combats proliferation of cancer and tumor cells

- anti-depressant / anxiolytic – eliminates depression and anxiety symptoms

- antioxidants- fights various neurodegenerative problems

Possible Health Risks and Side Effects of CBD

The safety when using CBD is the primary concern of most people. Naturally, many studies have looked into this matter thoroughly and found that it is relatively safe for most people to use—of course, this also depends on any existing allergies that they might have, along with conditions that might not work well with the effects of CBD.

As for the basics, there were no significant side effects on the central nervous system nor did it cause any mood swings for people who used it continuously.

The most common side effect, however, is tiredness and feelings of fatigue. Other effects that some users have experienced also include: changes in weight, appetite, mild case of diarrhea or gastrointestinal discomfort, sleeping difficulty, dizziness and dry mouth. Again, this does not happen to everyone—only a select few.

Stopping the use of CBD oil too quickly does bring about certain effects as well, many of which are similar to nicotine withdrawal symptoms. This includes: nausea, dizziness, irritability and fogginess. It is best to lower the dose and talk to your doctor to assist you during this period.

Studies are still being conducted if it is safe to use CBD as treatment for children.

Chapter 4: How CBD works in the body

You may wonder how cannabidoid enters the human cell and effectively binds to receptors. The process is intricate, yet efficient.

Cannabidoid passes through cell membranes and attaches itself to Fatty Acid Binding Proteins. This particular protein travels with lipid molecules and penetrates the interior of the cells. Interestingly, the same protein is responsible for Tetrahydrocannabinol (THC) transport, including the marijuana-like molecules produced by the brain – 2 AG and the Endocanabinoids Ananamide.

Once CBD is inside the cells, the fatty acid amide hydrolase (FAAH) begins breaking down the metabolic enzyme called Anandamide. FAAH is a vital component of the molecular life cycle of the cell.

The Endocannabinoid system and cannabinoids

The cannabinoids main target is the Endocannabinoid system or ECS. It is found in the central nervous system and in the brain. All mammals have this system in their bodies. ECS is the structural, molecular system which controls the body's reaction to normal psychological processes. This system in the body was first discovered in the late 1980s, and quickly became the subject of study because of its vital role in regulating homeostasis (general condition of balance). It corrects and mediates neural responses to help the body maintain its normal balance.

It is a signaling system which manages and controls the body's response to pain, sleep, hunger, stress, blood pressure, circadian rhythms, body temperature, moods, memory, fertility, metabolism, intestinal vitality, bone density and other vital functions. The Endocannabinoid system responds to natural endogenous cannabinoids which are manufactured by the body. The system can be manipulated to react to externally-induced cannabinoids to cure medical ailments—hence the effectiveness of CBD supplements.

Receptors of Endocannabinoid System and CBD

The Endocannabinoid system has millions of tiny receptor sites in almost all areas of the body. However, it only has two 2 main receptors which work to bind cannabinoids - CB1 and CB2.

CB1 receptors are found in the central nervous system and in the brain while **CB2** receptors are located in the immune system. They interact and work together through neural communication. The body's natural Endocannabinoids, the 2-AG and Anandamide control this cellular communication.

However, cannabidiol (CBD) from the cannabis hemp plant does not fit CB1 and CB2. *So how does it work when it enters the body?* CBD stimulates the receptor activities without binding itself to them. The result changes the cellular responses and can be systemic since CB1 and CB2 receptors are all over the body.

If THC is present in the system, CBD presence will counteract the known psychoactive effect of the compound on CB1 receptors.

Cytochrome P-450 System and CBD

Cannabidiol's ability to cure various illnesses can be done by manipulating the Endocannabinoid system. It is important for people to understand that CBD can be dangerous if improperly administered. CBD can inhibit the ability of *Cytochrome P-450 system* to metabolize medication for certain types of diseases. Cytochrome P-450 is a system found in the liver and is responsible for breaking down 90% of the drugs you take. This system has over 50 types of enzymes which process and flushes out toxins.

CBD presence in the system does prolong the processing of drugs and its effect on the body. This may also cause higher doses of drugs in the system, and if you're not careful, this can lead to an overdose or other adverse side-effects. It is vital to make dosage adjustments if you are taking both your medication drug and CBD.

Here are some of the drugs that utilize Cytochrome P-450 system which interact with cannabidiol (CBD):

- Antihistamines
- Antibiotics
- Steroids
- Anesthetics
- Benzodiazepines
- Calcium channel blockers
- Anti-psychotics
- Anti-depressants
- Anti-arrythmics
- Anti-epileptics
- Prokinetics
- Immune modulators
- Beta blockers
- HIV antivirals
- HMG CoA reductase inhibitors
- Sulfonylureas
- Angiotension II blockers
- Oral hypoglycemic agents
- PPIs
- NSAIDs

It is vital to consult your doctor before taking CBD dietary supplements so they can adjust the dosage for your other medications. While you are there, ask him to test your Cytochrome P-450 system to make sure that it is functioning excellently and metabolizing your medications as it should.

Other Effects of CBD

Cannabidiol can also affect the other functions of our bodies.

One of them is binding itself to G-protein coupled receptors (TRPV-1). This receptor regulates body inflammation, perceptions of pains and mediating body temperature.

It activates the receptors that stimulate serotonin.

And finally, its potent power inhibits the ID-1 gene which is responsible for the formation of aggressive types of cancers in brain, breast, pancreas, lungs and ovaries.

The Entourage Effect

In alternative medicine, the whole plant is utilized for medicinal use to gain its optimum benefits. Note that its plant form is known to be more effective for treating various medical conditions when compared to synthetic forms of substance.

The whole and cooperative effects of cannabinoids including terpenoids and flavonoids were observed by cannabis science pioneer Dr. Raphael Mechoulam and his team. They called it the "entourage effect."

"Entourage effect" is a phenomenon produced by the interaction of natural plant components with the body to bring more potent effects for treating a disease. The combined power of multiple and natural compounds has a multiplying effect which benefits the body. Every compound can amplify the ability of other compounds to bring over-all treatment of diseases.

Cannabis for instance has many active compounds which include the most popular- the cannabidiol (CBD) and the tetrahyrocannabinol (THC). These various forms of compounds in cannabis work together and alleviate negative symptoms. CBD can both modulate and neutralize THC effects on the body. When a person takes marijuana which contains high-amount of THC, this makes them feel "high". On the other hand, the hemp plant, which contains more cannabidiol (CBD), would instead bring relief to the body minus the psychoactive effect. Specially-bred cannabis marijuana has almost equal amounts of CBD and THC, and can be effectively used to alleviate pain and various other symptoms.

Terpene is another botanical component which is known to contain volatile molecules which easily evaporate. There are about 200 terpenes or terpenoids in cannabis plants although only few contain substantial amounts to be note-worthy, this includes: sesquiterpenes, diterpenes and monoterpenes. They contain isoprene or repeating 5-carbon molecule units.

One popular type of sesquitere is the beta-caryophyllene. It is the oil found in black pepper, oregano, several cannabis strains and many green, leafy vegetables. It can directly adhere or bind itself to CB2 or the peripheral cannabinoid receptors. This component helps protect the gastrointestinal tract and can also treat certain types of ulcer. It also offers potential promise as treatment for auto-immune disorders and inflammatory issues. The ability of beta-caryophyllene to easily bind itself to CB2 receptors makes it a "dietary cannabinoid."

The interaction of cannabinoids and terpenoids create potent synergy that kills active respiratory pathogens including the antibiotic-resistant MRSA bacteria. It also enhances cortical activity, increases blood circulation, and treats inflammation, anxiety, depression, cancer, epilepsy, addiction, pain, bacterial and fungal infections.

So why not use the entire plant?

Despite the above-mentioned benefits of using the whole plant, it is not feasible in many places, particularly in the US, because of the following reasons:

1. The botanical extracts' potency is not consistent due to weather and environmental conditions.

2. Because of the insufficient understanding of its components that bring therapeutic effects to the body, botanical products are not standardized.

3. The Food and Drug Administration (FDA) is not closely monitoring herbal products which can result to poor quality control. This can bring adulterated, contaminated, unsafe and less effective botanical products.

However, there are ongoing studies with the purpose of shedding more light on the capability of using whole plants to cure diseases and harnessing their full therapeutic potency.

The public become more aware of this *"entourage effect"* when Dr. Sanjay Gupta, a neurosurgeon and media personality wrote about it being effective to reduce spasms and pain of Multiple Sclerosis instead of medication containing single compound.

Clinical Endocannabinoid Deficiency Syndrome (CEDS)

CEDS is the medical term for one group of diseases which includes: fibromyalgia, irritable bowel syndrome and migraine. According to various scientists and medical experts, these illnesses are caused by low endocannabinoid level in the body.

The level of endocannabinoids can affect the proper functioning of some body systems. Very low endocannabinoid level brings active CEDS symptoms. One significant study regarding CEDS found that Anandamide receptors are directly affected by insufficient amount of endocannabinoids in the body. These receptors are closely linked to periaqueductal gray matter otherwise known as "migraine generator" of the human brain. This endocannabinoid deficiency can trigger symptoms of migraine and other conditions under CEDS. Increased and sufficient level stops adverse gastrointestinal, peripheral and spinal actions.

To overcome this condition, you would need to increase your Omega-3 fatty acid intake. This will also increase the production of natural endogenous cannabinoids. It also heals and facilitates growth of your CB1 receptors.

Taking CBD or cannabidiol to supplement the endogenous cannabinoids of the body helps to correct the deficiency. It leads to more active and efficient endocannabinoid system.

Chapter 5: CBD Hemp Oil

One of the fastest-growing products in the oil industry is the Cannabidiol hemp oil (CBD hemp oil). It has become a highly-demanded oil in more than 40 countries and 50 states of United States.

Cannabidiol hemp oil became widely sought after a highly-publicized media exposure. It has taken the general public by storm after Dr. Sanjay Gupta presented a television special documentary called "Weed" in CNN. He investigated and documented the ability of cannabidoid to treat children suffering from epilepsy.

The initial purpose is to view it as medicine for critically-ill patients, but the general public's interest kept on growing and more studies have since been made into just how beneficial it can be for treating different illnesses as well as for boosting a person's overall health. There was an instant demand and people were looking for place where they could buy CBD hemp oil. Grocery stores, doctor's clinics and medical marijuana dispensaries started displaying CBD hemp oil. Purchasing the product is easy and does not require medical card.

The oil is extracted from seeds and stalk of industrial hemp plant. It contains large quantity of CBD or cannabidiol compounds. However, the extraction process must also ensure that it produces highly-concentrated CBD oil and doesn't change it in any way. The oil is also abundant with other nutrients like vitamins, amino acids, Omega-3 fatty acids, chlorophyll, terpenes, and phytocannabinoids such as cannabidivarian (CBCV), canabicromene (CBD), cannabinol (CBN) and cannabigerol (CBG).

Full-Spectrum Hemp Oil

Full-spectrum refers to a hemp oil that is pure and concentrated. It contains the same amount and quality of compounds and cannabinoids of the source plant. Unlike synthetic products, this type of hemp oil has a dozen forms of cannabinoids plus vitamins, minerals, protein, fatty acids, chlorophyll, fiber, terpenes and flavonoids.

Cannabinoids

Full spectrum hemp oil contains abundant supply of cannabidiol (CBD). It amounts to more than 90% of total cannabinoids. Hemp oil has cannabinoid cannabidiolic acid (CBDa) which turns into CBD compound during heating process or decarboxylation. Aside from CBD, full-spectrum hemp oil has other major forms of cannabinoids such as tetrahydrocannabinol (THC), cannabinol (CBN) and cannabigerol (CBG).

Vitamins and Minerals

Full-spectrum hemp oil has great quantity of essential vitamins A, C, E and B-complex vitamins (niacin, riboflavin and thiamine). It is also a good source of beta-carotene and other forms of vitamins which are not abundantly available in daily diets.

Minerals such as iron, zinc, calcium, magnesium, potassium and phosphorous can be found from full-spectrum hemp oil. These minerals are vital for metabolic processes, bodily functions, nerve functions, building strong bones, and healthy skin, skin and blood circulation.

Essential Proteins and Fats

Protein is the building block of muscles. It repairs tissues and cells. Hemp oil contains 9 essential amino acids and 11 others which are all important for body functions.

Fatty acids are important compounds to sustain cardiovascular health and excellent heart condition. Full-spectrum hemp oil has essential fatty acids like Omega-3 and Omega-6.

CBD Hemp Oil versus Hemp Oil

Be mindful that CBD hemp oil is different from organic hemp oil that is commercially available in grocery stores.

Hemp oil or hempseed oil does not have cannabidiol. However, it contains vitamins, minerals and other nutrients. It is produced by pressing the seeds of hemp. Unrefined and cold-pressed hemp oil has nutty flavor and has a dark green to light green color. The darker the color, the grassier the taste. It is rich in omega-3 to omega-6 fatty acids. The nutritional value is about 1:3 which matches the body's requirement.

Refined hemp oil is colorless with little flavor. It does not have natural nutrients such as vitamins and lacks antioxidant properties. The refined form is usually utilized as ingredients for body care essentials such as soaps and shampoos. It is also used in detergents. Industrial hemp oil is commonly used for plastics, lubricants, fuel, paints and inks. It has a subject of studies as potential feedstock to produce biodiesel in large-scale level.

Hempseed oil comes from Cannabis sativa varieties which do not have high components of tetrahydrocannabinol (THC). There is no THC element in hempseed. The traces that are found present in hemp oil can be due to adherence of plant matter to seed surface when it is manufactured. In Canada, the manufacturers successfully lowered THC content when they started using more modern production methods back in 1998. Sampling showed 4ppm or parts per million (4 mg.kg.) which is below the 10 ppm detection limit. Other countries in Europe impose 5ppm to none detection limit.

On the other hand, CBD hemp oil is a botanical, highly-concentrated and pure form of cannabidiol. It is extracted from the stalks, leaves and flowers. It supports general health and well-being. It is also non-addictive and safe to use. Its potency to bring therapeutic benefits is now widely-known. Hemp CBD dietary supplements are regulated by the FDA.

Methods of CBD Hemp Oil Extraction

There are three methods to extract this valuable oil from hemp plants.

1. Oil Method – It is the most popular way to produce oil from industrial hemp. It uses carrier oils, such as olive oil, for the process. The combined power of CBD hemp oil and carrier oil brings greater benefits to users. It also prevents unwanted residues and guarantees safety.

2. CO_2 Method – The procedure involves pushing CO_2 out of hemp at high pressure levels and low temperature. The process results to a pure form of CBD. It is considered the safest and the best way to extract the oil because it removes unwanted substances like chlorophyll and does not leave unsafe residues. It also produces a cleaner taste, but the process is expensive.

This process requires equipment that can force the

cannabinoid solution and CO_2 to separate from each other. During this, the cannabinoids would go to different chambers than the CO_2. Manufacturers like this process because it enables them to "customize" the resulting product.

3. Ethanol Method – This process of oil extraction involves the use of high-grain alcohol which can destroy the natural oils elements.

Rick Simpson was the originator of using alcohol to extract an "original" or purer type of CBD oil. He soaked hemp material in a solvent and after a while, it produced liquid which is full of cannabidoids. He then evaporated the solvent to leave only the essential liquid.

His method was copied and used by large-scale manufacturers to produce commercially-available CBD hemp oil products. The alcohol solution that is left behind is put through "Roto-Vap" which separates ethanol from the oil. The alcohol goes to another chamber instead of evaporating and the machine stores it for future use. The oil that is left is ready for users' consumption.

How to produce your own CBD

You can produce your own CBD or cannabidoids at home using simple and safe techniques. You do not need special skills or expensive equipment to make your own oil.

What you need

- 30 grams of ground hemp buds (60-100 ground of ground, dried trim)

- 4l grain alcohol (any high-proof and food-safe alcohol) Grain alcohol is the best option because it doesn't leave any unpleasant and harmful residue. It is an excellent solvent for extracting small batches of cannabis oil.

- ceramic (or glass) mixing bowl

- fine strainer (sieve, cheesecloth, nylon stocking)

- double boiler (or set of 2 pots/saucepans with space in between when they are stacked together)

- catchment container

- silicon spatula

- plastic syringe

- wooden spoon

- funnel

Procedure

- Start by setting up your tools.

- Place the hemp material in the mixing bowl, then put grain alcohol and stir the solution for 3-5 minutes using wooden spoon.

- Mix thoroughly to expel resin. Make sure that your mixing bowl is large enough to contain the plant material and solvent.

- Next, filter the solution into the drainer then collect the initial raw extraction and placed it in the catchment container. Squeeze the liquid.

- Transfer the collected liquid to the double burner and heat it. Wait until it bubbles. Allow the alcohol to evaporate. Keep the temperature at minimal level. You can also turn it on and off to keep the gentle bubbling of the solution for 15-30 minutes.

- Stir regularly. Do not allow the solution to be too hot. When you see alcohol evaporating, carefully mix the liquid using the silicon spatula.

- Your solution is ready. Transfer the oil to a bottle or containers before it becomes thick. Use a plastic syringe or pour the concentrated CBD oil to small, airtight and dark dosage bottles.

*While still warm, dilute the concentrated extract with coconut oil, olive oil or vegetable oil of your choice to make excellent ointment for topical use.

Chapter 6: Different Types of CBD Hemp Oil

CBD and THC act on different enzymes and receptors. Using CBD infused products can effectively counteract the effects of THC like over-excitability and paranoia. It is 100% non-psychoactive, non-addictive and safe.

Hemp oil products can be purchased legally in any part of America and other countries across the globe including: Argentina, Austria, Belgium, Belize, Brazil, Bulgaria, Canada, Chile, China, Colombia, Costa Rica, Croatia, Cyprus, Czech Republic, Denmark, England, Estonia, Finland, France, Georgia, Germany, Greece, Guam, Guatemala, Hong Kong, Hungary, Iceland, India, Ireland, Italy, Latvia, Lithuania, Luxembourg, Malta, Netherlands, Netherlands Antilles, Northern Ireland, Norway, Paraguay, Peru, Poland, Portugal, Puerto Rico, Romania, Russia, Scotland, Slovak Republic, Slovenia, South Africa, Sweden, Switzerland, U.S. Virgin Islands, United Kingdom, Uruguay and Wales.

There are various forms and concentrations of CBD. These include liquid hemp oil, oil in capsules, hemp oil in thick paste form, sprays or sublingual tincture drops, CBD vaporizers (vapes), concentrates, salves for topical application and edibles (gum or candy).

When taken orally, it is necessary to hold the solution under your tongue to allow direct absorption before swallowing it. This step is important because the digestive system can break the CBD down once it reaches the stomach.

CBD hemp oil, when taken at lower dosages, relaxes and calms the body.

Tinctures

Tincture is a liquid extract intended for oral use. The exact amount of CBD solution is measured by the product's dropper top. It is the most common form of CBD laden product. It is the purest application since manufacturers do not use separation methods to extract the oil. There are brands which have a little flavor which is helpful for consumers who do like a little taste during consumption.

It is considered to be the most effective way to gain the benefits of CBD. Its ability to bring precise dosages ensures optimum benefit. It is also very easy to increase or decrease the quantity you take.

You can also opt to mix the CBD tincture with your favorite drink while on the go. The recommended dose is from 100mg-1000mg. It is vital to know your needs or start slow and gradually increase the dosage to find the strength you need.

There are many flavors available in the market today. CBD tinctures are now flavored with vanilla, cinnamon, peppermint and many more. Others have sweeteners to make them tastier.

The downside of using tinctures is messiness if you spill some of it during usage but this is just a minor issue.

How to apply

Shake the solution well. Separation of oil with the other elements of the product is natural when it is not used. Shaking it blends all the helpful ingredients of the solution and neutralizes the strong taste.

Use the dropper top and fill the pipette then dispense 2 drops of oil under your tongue. Swish it around your mouth or let it sit for 30-90 seconds to allow your system to fully absorb the oil.

If the taste is too strong for you, drink juice or apple cider to neutralize the hempy flavor as you ingest it. Repeat when needed throughout the whole day.

Concentrates or Oil Form

This form is the most popular among users who want a more potent form of CBD. This contains high-dosages of cannabidiol. Typically, 10 times stronger compared to other types. It is more convenient to use. CBD concentrates have little to no flavor for those who do not want the bland taste of oil.

The downside is its inability to be flavored. It can be a big deal for people who cannot take natural flavors and are unable to swallow down the oil. For beginners, concentrates can be a little shocking because their shapes are like syringes.

How to apply

Like tincture, placing it under the tongue and ingesting it slowly is the way to consume it.

Sprays

This is the weakest form of CBD when it comes to concentration. The typical CBD concentration usually amounts anywhere from 1-3 mg. It is difficult to measure the right dosage because spray is a little bit inconsistent.

One of the advantages of using spray is convenience and it can be used whenever needed. It is easier to spray CBD oil into the mouth compared to using concentrate or tincture if you are on a travel.

How to apply

Spray one dosage CBD oil into your mouth. The right dosage should be on the bottle label. The typical instruction is 2-3 sprays daily or as needed.

Capsules

Taking in CBD oil in capsule form is the easiest method if you're using it as a daily supplement. It is usually packaged in dissolvable capsules with high CBD concentration. It is odorless and tasteless. It works well with other supplements like vitamins or minerals. Each package contains 2-60 capsules. It makes measuring or tracking down your daily dosage easier. When in doubt, it is easy to know if you are able to take your daily dose by counting the remaining capsules.

One downside of CBD capsule is when you want to up your dosage by a bit but you don't' want to swallow 2 capsules. One way to address this concern is to add other forms of CBD product such as tincture to adjust your serving size every day.

How to apply

Take one capsule a day or as needed.

Topical

Many topical brands in the market now are laden with CBD. This includes: lip balms, creams lotions and salves. Products with CBD help in anti-aging, inflammation, cancer treatment, chronic pain, psoriasis and acne. The topical products have unique usability which includes targeting specific areas of inflammation or stiffness in the body. Topical CBD products are easily-absorbed and can be used to directly alleviate pain and discomfort of the body zones.

When selecting topical products, check the following keywords which indicate that it uses CBD- encapsulation: **micellization and nano technology**. These indicators are proof that the product can penetrate easily through the skin's dermal layer and makes CBD work not just on the outer skin, but also deep within.

However, because topical products by skin absorption, it does have a tendency to work slower compared to other forms of CBD products. The products –lotions, balms and creams are also more expensive because they are infused with high-quality ingredients aside from cannabidiol.

How to apply

Like any other topical body care products, apply it generously to affected area of the body. Use it as often as necessary.

Vaporizers

Smoking CBD or vaporizing CBD oil helps the user adjust the dosage that's right for them. Think of it as being very similar to an e-cigarette or e-pen. The CBD oil is heated up into a vapor before it can be inhaled. The vaporizing methods works fast and is also safe for the oral tract because. Note that vaporizers do not produce smoke.

When purchasing vaporizers, you will receive two products – the vaporizer and CBD cartridges which contain the oil. Vaporizes are convenient, handy, lightweight and a stylish form of using CBD.

It has lesser drawback compared to taking CBD products orally. Concentrates, tinctures and capsules take a longer period to be absorbed which brings delayed effect.

How to apply

You need vaporizer, inhaler, e-cigarette or vape pen. Add appropriate amount of CBD hemp oil to your device, heat and inhale.

Edibles

Nowadays, CBD can be excellently lumped into variety of edibles.

> *Chocolate bar* - One of the most popular edible forms is a CBD laden bar of chocolate. It offers many great benefits and is also very easy to consume. It also masks the distinct hempy taste. Chocolate bars allows you to effectively control the dosage you take. It is a more discreet way of taking CBD.

Most CBD chocolate bars are infused with about 10mg of hemp oil. If this is your desired amount, you can consume it at once or take smaller bites throughout the day. There are also variety of flavors – dark chocolate, mint dark chocolate, Raspberry Milk chocolate and more.

CBD Gums/Chews

There are gums or chews with CBD oil. These edible products promote instant calm. CBD can also be combined effectively with other elements like essential vitamins, caffeine and flavors to enhance the benefits of the product.

1 piece of gum/chew taken as necessary is recommended.

CBD Lozenges

Lozenges with CBD are refreshingly good because of their minty taste. Most brands offer sugar-free, gluten free, dairy free products and preservative-free for consumers who have special dietary needs.

It is easy to use lozenges. Just pop one into your mouth. It is best taken on an empty stomach. 1-2 lozenges a day is the recommended serving for optimum CBD absorption.

CBD Dab Oils or Wax

To produce wax, solvent is used during extraction process. Using vape pens, it is applied through dabbing. It instantly help with reducing chronic pain, inflammation and anxiety. It produces potent relief with just 2-3 strokes of vape pen.

Gel Pen

It gently soothes and offers lasting relief when applied to affected area of the body. Gel pens are perfect for patients who suffer from consistent chronic pains. It is safe to use and does not bring adverse side effects. It is also light to carry anywhere.

The best method of using this is to put an amount of gel to areas with superficial veins like temples, wrists or ankles (or any part where you can clearly see your veins). Gently press the pen's tip on the spot then spread the gel for maximum absorption. It usually works within 15-20 minutes upon application. If you are unsure of the appropriate amount that would work for you, can start with a small amount then increase it gradually to get the desired result you need.

Do not use if you are lactating or pregnant. For patients with chronic illness or taking regular medication, consult your doctor first to know if it is safe for you to use CBD gel pens.

Always keep the product in dry, cool place. Secure it away from pets and little children.

CBD Patches

Patches are infused with CBD are therapeutic. Most brands would contain 2.5mg of pure CBD and no THC. You can use it at once or cut it to spread the dosage within the day. It is best for users with anxiety issues and fibromyalgia condition.

It works after 15-20 minutes. The sensation it brings is mild and does not interfere with regular daily tasks. After 45 to an hour, the curing sensation stops and leaves you feeling better. It brings physical and mental relief for the next hours.

Chapter 7: How to Use CBD Hemp Oil

The prime source of CBD oil is hemp or industrial hemp. CBD oil is a natural, concentrated, non-psychoactive extract from hemp plant which contains low-THC and high-CBD components. At present, there are many brands, types and forms of CBD hemp oil that are available for both skin care and dietary needs.

Pure CBD hemp oil can also be taken directly as dietary or nutritional supplement. Its concentrated form can be used topically or infused into body and skin care products. The therapeutic and beauty benefits of CBD oil gave rise to various product forms – drops, capsules and chewing gum.

The many benefits of CBD hemp oil has certainly changed public opinion about it. The once-taboo herb is now more associated with supplemental nutrition values. The potential of cannabidiol hemp oil to address the nutritional needs of consumers brought it to public awareness. There were about 23,000 published studies in various medical journals giving information about the good benefits of cannabis oil and cannabinoids in human body without the "high" effect.

With increased interest in CBD hemp oil, it is important to understand how this oil can help the nutritional requirements of consumers.

Because there is no scientifically-proven and recommended dosing regimen, it is important to do it step-by-step. Begin at small dosage then gradually adjust the concentration to address your specific need. Every product has recommended daily serving which you can follow. However, it is best to do some studies regarding hemp oil so you would know how much dosage you need and how often.

Dietary Supplements

CBD hemp oil has variety of concentrated forms, ranging in amount anywhere from 1 mg/serving up to 80 mg/serving. The wide range of CBD concentration is helpful for those who want to maximize their usage to suit their purposes. All dietary supplements have clear instructions with suggested serving doses and the CBD amount per serving.

A little amount of CBD can greatly benefit a user. If it is your first time to use CBD dietary supplements, it is best to start with a low concentration then slowly increase the dosage along the way. You can also speak to your physician about what might be the right amount for you depending on what you're using for, as well as if you're taking other supplements at the moment.

Methods of CBD Hemp Oil Consumption

There are several factors that influence the impact of CBD on human health. It includes dosage, mode of consumption and symptoms of the medical trouble.

- Vape – It is the most convenient, efficient and safest way.

- Sublingual – It produces fast relief within few minutes.

- Topical – It the slowest and you need to apply uniform amount of CBD hemp oil to ensure optimum result.

- Orally – It takes about 30-60 minutes to feel the result. It is best taken on empty stomach.

- Add-on to food or drink – It help cure headaches and dysphoria. Although, it takes long time to feel the effect, it guarantees no adverse side effects.

What is The Standard Amount?

Many doctors, when asked for CBD supplement prescriptions are reluctant because there is no guiding prescription available. Pharmacology courses do not tackle CBD's proper dosage. Medical scientists are only beginning to develop dosing schedules for the medical use of hemp extracts and medical marijuana.

Different brands offer different standards of CBD dosage which can be very confusing for many people, especially for first time users.

CBDOilReview.org (COR) provided simple standard which you can consider. It recommends CBD serving of 25mg twice within the day. You can gradually increase your consumption by 25mg every 3-4 weeks. If side effects manifest during consumption, decrease the dosage.

General guidelines for CBD Hemp Oil Usage for Treatment:

- Chronic Pain

    2.5- 20 mg by mouth for 25 days

- Epilepsy

    200 – 300 mg by mouth every day for 4 ½ months

- Sleep Disorders/Insomia

    40-160 mg by mouth when needed

- Huntington's disease

    To ease movement problem, take 10 mg/kilogram by mouth every day for 1 ½ months

- Schizophrenia

  40- 1,280 mg by mouth every day for up to one month

- Multiple Sclerosis Symptoms

  2.5 -120 mg of CBD-THC combination by mouth every day from 2-15 weeks. Mouth spray containing the compounds is given to patients up to 8 weeks. A maximum of 48 sprays per day or 8 sprays every 3 hours is recommended to maximize the benefits.

- Glaucoma

  20-40 mg placed under tongue every day. More than 40 mg dosage is dangerous because it increases eye pressure.

There is no recorded case of lethal CBD dose. But, consumers must follow the instructions thoroughly to find the right dosage and maximize its effects. It is highly important to talk to your physician and get prescription from him before taking CBD supplements.

Chapter 8: Guide for Buying CBD Hemp Oil

At this point in time, you may be wondering about where to buy and how to buy CBD hemp oil and other CBD products. In this chapter, we breakdown all the information you need to know.

Initially, you would need to consider the best CBD brand, the concentration of CBD, the type of CBD product and your particular purpose or need for the product. CBD products come in different forms, shapes and sizes. Comparing and distinguishing which among the almost similar products is best for you is necessary before making a final decision.

- *CBD Volume*

    Find out the amount of CBD in each product. Different brands and products offer varying CBD content. To find out the quantity, make sure that the product specifically refers to CBD and not the overall quantity of hemp oil.

    CBD product is typically measured using two quantities – CBD quantity and Hemp Oil quantity (total volume of oil content). Always check for CBD quantity in the label.

- *CBD Concentration*

Concentration is another essential characteristic that you need to look for in CBD hemp oil product. This determines how much cannabidiol in the product. Amounts can vary anywhere from: normal strength to super-high CBD concentration or hundred percent pure natural concentration ranges.

CBD concentration would aid you in finding the right dosage you need to maximize the benefit. It is recommended for adult beginners to take small doses of about 1-3mg every day. Gradually, you can adjust the size of serving once the body becomes accustomed with the substance. You can double the amount the week after your first try or adjust the quantity to find the accurate quantity your body specifically needs. Because CBD does not have psychoactive effects, you can safely take optimal concentration to gain its benefits just like what multi-vitamins supplements do to the body.

- *Types of CBD products*

CBD hemp oil is a versatile substance which can be effectively turned into different types of products – from capsules, tinctures, vaporizers and more. Whatever form it takes, the health benefits that it offers remain potent. However, different brands offer different concentrations, flavors and method of consumption (there are CBD hemp oils that are designed to be added to drinks or foods while others are produced for synergistic effects).

Other factors that you need to consider before buying CBD hemp oil are:

- *Manufacturer/Distributor Track Record*

  It is essential to do basic research first and look for a company that has a reliable track record. Read reviews regarding the company and find out users' comments about their experience with buying from the company. It is important to make sure that you purchase high-quality, effective and safe CBD hemp oil. Despite being a new industry in the market, there are already established brands out there that would be able to provide you with quality products.

- *Clear Labeling Design*

  It is vital to get a product that provides you with a proper label, one that outlines all the ingredients of the product. It must clearly show other essential details such as expected shelf life, standard serving size and proper storage method.

- *Avoidance of Health Claims*

  CBD hemp oil in United States is categorized under dietary supplements. Any company that claims its ability to cure any medical case is violating FDA's DSHEA rules and regulation.

Where to buy CBD Hemp Oil

The importation of CBD hemp oil and other dietary supplements that contains CBD is now legal. It is easy to purchase the product online in over 40 manufacturing countries around the world.

It is readily available for consumers who want to try the effectiveness of CBD in addressing different health concerns. CBD hemp oil products can be bought in online stores, medical marijuana dispensaries and in various wellness or natural products stores.

When buying CBD hemp oil, always check for quality and try to avoid low-priced brands. Do not be tempted by affordability, always focus on its quality even if it means you have to pay a little extra. CBD quality is measured by the quantity of the cannabidiol concentration that the product contains. The higher the concentration, the more potent its effects would be.

Chapter 9: Is CBD Hemp Oil Good for Pets?

According to scientific studies, all animals except insects produce endocabinnoids. The presence of endocabinnoid system in animal bodies helps them regulate their physiological responses. Like humans, there are receptors throughout their bodies that can be activated by inducing phytocannabinoids-- in particular cannabidoid (CBD. CBD can effectively cure the underlying symptoms of disease among animals in a more natural way.

So, is it safe to give your dog or pets?

The answer is yes. Based on research and experiments conducted by scientists, CBD also benefits animals. CBD was first mixed with edible canine treats and were given to animals who were suffering from pain, inflammation and cancer-related issues—this showed positive results. CBD can also be utilized for fatal ailments or palliative care.

Pets, especially dogs, who are suffering from severe arthritis or inoperable cancer experience muscle wasting and usually have no appetite. CBD can help with that as well. In using it, pet owners can also avoid the risk of damaging their pet's kidney and liver which happens due to constant use of synthetic medication.

CBD contains very low THC so it will not make your pet high. One common side effect of cannabidiol, however, is drowsiness which is not dangerous. Other rare side effects are mild vomiting and itchiness.

Can it be used to treat chronic and acute conditions?

CBD is beneficial to pets suffering from acute and chronic diseases. Chronic conditions include: aggression, compromised immune system, digestive issues, osteoarthritis and stress. There are also ongoing studies if cannabidiol can effectively treat different canine cancers, Type 1 diabetes and organ diseases.

Cannabidiol (CBD) treatments have also been found to be beneficial for treating acute ailments such as bone breakage, strains and sprains, torn ligaments and post-operative issues like stiffness, swelling and pain.

Pet owners who do not want to see their canine pets suffering are looking for ways to provide them with relief and ease the pain their beloved pets are feeling. CBD can help with this as well. Furthermore, it is known to soothe pet anxiety-- especially during veterinary visits, fear from thunderstorm, separation anxiety, social anxiety and traveling in cars. These vouched the ability of CBD to help canine pets and their owners.

Why are veterinarians cautious when prescribing CBD?

Despite the benefits of CBD induced treatment, it is not yet prescribed by most veterinarians. They refrain from endorsing cannabis plant extracts due to two reasons.

First: Issues with misinformation and pet owners using actual cannabis in treating their pets. These concerns are validated when recreational cannabis was legalized in different states including Colorado. Many dogs suffered from marijuana poisoning caused by large consumption of cannabis which contains high amounts of THC. Dogs would often suffer seizures then go into coma and eventually die.

Second: The lack of understanding and awareness of non-psychoactive cannabinoids like CBD. Many veterinarians still have a predominant view that cannabis is a toxic plant. Sad to say, there are still large numbers of vets who are unaware that cannabis has different strains and most of them do not produce psychoactive effects.

There is also a clout of doubt that many veterinarians are resisting CBD induced treatments because this may affect the multi-billion dollar pet medication industry. As of 2013, the Federal Trade Commission reported a $ 7.6 billion sales and expected to balloon to $10.2 billion dollars in 2018.

Does CBD work fast even for pets?

Cannabidiol is a botanical or herbal drug which does not bring instant effects. It usually takes two hours to be fully ingested an absorbed to their system. However, it can arrest pain within few minutes but you will need to wait longer for inflammation and other underlying symptoms to heal.

Is CBD metabolism among dogs similar to humans?

The answer is no. Dogs metabolize cannabidiol in different way. Do you remember the anandamide and 2-AG compounds? These two natural chemicals are produced by the human body and are also present in canines as well. These 2 chemicals activate and trigger CB1 and CB2 receptors in canines. CBD tend to bind these 2 receptors for a longer period thus creating long-lasting therapeutic benefits for dogs without causing any toxic effect.

During intravenous infusions conducted to see the effect of cannabidiol in canines, there was a rapid response which is followed with 9-hour terminal half-life. It caused low oral bioavailability of about 13-19%. This also helps eliminate systemic toxicity among dogs. After the effects wane, the CBD is metabolized by the dog's liver and flushes it out of the body naturally. This can be the reason of immediate and long-lasting effects of CBD to diseased animals.

So what do the different studies reveal?

Studies supporting cannabinoid use among for animals showed that CBD was able to improve their mobility. It also improved their pet's appetite and successfully reduced their tendency to rely on traditional synthetic veterinary drugs. Most canines actually develop an intolerance to these drugs.

Another study showed that cannabinoids can effectively prevent inflammatory allergic problems, skin diseases and immune-mediated health issues in pets. CBD also has higher level of anti-epileptic and anticonvulsant properties compared to conventional drugs that are used to treat these conditions.

Other studies show that the following medical conditions were successfully relieved using edible CBD treats – pain, inflammation, nausea or vomiting, nervous system problems, anxiety, tumors, convulsions, seizures, digestive system disorders, phobias and skin problems.

CBD is also beneficial for canines suffering from osteoarthritis (OA) that causes neuropathic pain.

What other animals can benefit from cannabidoid (CBD)?

Aside from dogs, the other mammal with an endocannabinoid system is the mice. Invertebrate and vertebrate species like cats, chicken, turtles, sea urchin and fish also have cannabinoid receptors that respond to phytocannabinoids.

However, there are distinct differences in the cannabinoid systems of these species. Rodents like mice and rats have cannabinoid receptors that are mostly located along the brain's cerebellum and basal ganglia. These areas control their body movements and coordination. Humans, in comparison, have a lower concentration of receptors in these areas.

One of the most common neurological disorders among dogs is epilepsy. Studies reveal that epileptic dogs have high level of endocannabidoids in their endocannabinoid system. This is because these compounds are attempting to combat seizures caused by the disease. Another answer is the possibility that seizures damaged the normal functioning of the endocannabinoid system and caused higher levels of endocannabinoid production in their bodies.

What is the proper dosage for dogs?

Different types of health conditions among dogs need different dosages. It is best to start with a low dosage of CBD hemp oil then gradually adjust to the recommended amount. This way can help your dog's body gets accustomed with its effects.

One recommended method is giving 1 drop per 10 pounds of your dog's weight every day for about one week. Then, give it 1 drop twice a day during the second week until you manage to find the proper dosage that gives relief and cures the illness of your dog minus the side effects.

If they aren't showing any side effects, you can continue increasing the amount of CBD oil every 4-5 days until such time you clearly see the therapeutic benefits of cannabidiol (CBD). When there is any presence of side effects such as vomiting, disorientation, excessive sedation and hyperactivity, stop CBD treatment and allow them to pass. After some time, begin again with lower dose.

If you are using CBD treats like cookies, be sure not to exceed the maximum recommended amount in the instruction. A quarter of a piece at the beginning is best for your pets. Avoid handing CBD treats like regular food treats. Store them in place where your pets cannot easily access them.

<u>Things to remember when purchasing CBD treats for your dogs:</u>

First, use products that are especially formulated for the type of pet you have.

Second, choose which form of CBD you think will benefit your pets the most. CBD products come in tincture or oil form and food treats. Tinctures are the most common method to administer CBD oil to your dog. Putting the oil directly into your pet's mouth can be messy so you can choose to use treats.

Third, many online stores are selling CBD products for pets. To make sure that you are getting a product that's legitimate, you can choose to buy directly from manufacturers or their authorized stores.

Conclusion

Understanding how cannabidiol or CBD works to help sustain health and freedom from chronic to acute diseases is empowering. It helps consumers find answers to some of the most common health concerns which are often overlooked. Learning that the answer is simple and accessible makes it easy for everyone to find natural medications which are not only safe, but also effective in combating the symptoms of illnesses that can be debilitating as time goes on.

Pure botanical phytocannabinoids including CBD have proven their health benefits and has since become the subject of many studies. This injected life back into the hemp industry into the market, something that benefits not just its users, but the people who grow them as well.

With more published works being released and reflecting positive views on this beneficial plant, people are learning that it isn't something that's wholly bad—that there is a very distinct difference between the marijuana and hemp plant. A difference that they could take advantage of if they opt to educate themselves further on how to use hemp to better their overall health.

Despite the challenges of being classified as illegal because of the negative reputation of cannabis marijuana, CBD producing industrial hemp reemerged and carved its good reputation to the new world. It is showing its versatility and usability to combat health issues among humans and even their beloved canine companions.

It really pays to educate oneself on natural alternatives to the medication we usually take—all it takes is an open-mind, and the willingness to try new things. Who knows? This might be the very solution you've been looking for.

Thank you!

Before you go, I just wanted to say thank you for purchasing my book.

You could have picked from dozens of other books on the same topic but you took a chance and chose this one.

So, a HUGE thanks to you for getting this book and for reading all the way to the end.

Now I wanted to ask you for a small favor. **Could you please take just a few minutes to leave a review for this book?**

This feedback will help us continue to write the type of books that will help you get the results you want. So if you enjoyed it, please let us know! (-: